Seazar and Cleo's Pet Food Cookbook

S.E.B.'S

MARKETPLACE

All rights reserved

For additional Copies Write to:

**S.E.B.'S Marketplace
16 Wentworth Terrace
Dover, NH 03820**

Written and Illustrated by

S.E.B.'S Marketplace

File No. 219006

Form No. TN-2

R.S.A. 349:7

Printed in the USA by

MORRIS PUBLISHING

3212 East Highway 30 • Kearney, NE 68847 • 1-800-650-7888

TABLE OF CONTENTS

Dedicated to the Memory of:

Bootsey
Cindy
Fino
Frisky
Joshi
KC
Kristy
Lady
Lazaro
Little Girl
Melba
Mitten
Nanook
Sam
Smudge
Timmy
Tina

We also dedicate this book to all people who have the courage, time and heart to feed their pets the best way they are able.

Please support your local S.P.C.A. or local shelter

RECIPES

HOW YOU CAN MAKE YOUR OWN PET FOOD

As a pet owner, no doubt you want to give your dog or cat the best care possible, and caring for your pet means feeding him the best diet you can. Animals, because they are color blind, choose their foods by smell.

Most dogs like gamy flavors best, as well as liver, fat, garlic, onions, horsemeat, lamb, beef, cheese and fish.

Cats enjoy chicken, liver, fish, turkey, lamb, and yeast, and prefer fresh to aged flavors. Remember that cats are fussy eaters and it is not wise to continually feed them their favorite foods. Soon they will refuse to eat anything else; it is your job to see your cat has a balanced diet.

Animals do not need salt added to their diet as the natural salt in the food is enough for them.

Dogs may eat any vegetable they want, but cats should not have any starchy veggies like peas and corn. Some dogs and cats even enjoy fruits!

It's a good idea to always add a grain, such as Kibble, wheat germ, cooked oatmeal, or whole wheat bread to meat dinners.

For dogs use 75% carbohydrate foods (grains and vegetables) to 25% meat; for cats use half carbohydrate foods to half meat.

You will find, that once you begin making your own pet foods, that it is really relatively simple and you will save some money as well. Remember that all pet foods should be served at room temperature; don't serve food cold from the refrigerator, nor hot from the stove. Incidentally, you should know that cats should be fed three times a day, while an adult dog needs only one meal a day.

What's On the Menu?

Biscuits...........

Bacon
Beef
Cheese
Chicken
Garlic
Glazed
Liver
Meaty
Nutty
Variations
Veggie
Wheat, Whole Grains, Other Flours

Here are some pet recipes you can make at home:

Sautéed Liver

1 tsp. corn oil
1/4 lb. beef liver
1/2 cup water

Heat corn oil in a pan. Add beef liver and fry on both sides until cooked but not dry inside. Add water to the pan and mix it up with all the brown bits.

For dogs, cut the liver into pieces and serve; for cats, grind the liver in a blender, using the pan juices.

Chicken Soup

1 cup chicken liver
1 lb. giblet
1 chicken heart
1 chicken neck

2 cups water
1 tbsp. finely chopped parsley

Combine the chicken liver, giblet, chicken heart, chicken neck, water and finely chopped parsley. Cover and simmer until the giblet is tender.

Chop all the meat for dogs removing bones and mix with kibble; for cats, you may want to grind the meat in the blender.

Veal Stew

1/2 lb. stewing veal
1 cup canned tomatoes
1 cup water
1 chicken bouillon cube

1/2 cup onion (chopped)
1 tbsp. parsley
1 tbsp. garlic powder

Combine the veal, canned tomatoes, water, chicken bouillon cube, onion, parsley and a dash of garlic powder in a pot and simmer. When meat is tender, remove all the bones.

For dogs, cut the meat in chunks, and mix stew with kibble or some other grain; for cats, grind the stew in blender, adding a tablespoon of wheat germ or 1/2 slice of whole wheat bread.

Lamb Stew

Follow the recipe for Veal Stew, using chunks of lamb instead and leaving out the tomato if desired.

Liver Cookies

1/2 cup dry milk
1/2 cup wheat germ
1 tsp. honey
1 1/3 oz. jar strained liver baby food or homemade blended liver

Preheat oven to 350 degrees. Combine dry milk and wheat germ; drizzle teaspoon honey on top. Add the jar of strained liver baby food or homemade blended liver and stir until everything is well mixed. Form the mixture into balls; place them on a greased cookie sheet and flatten them with a fork. Bake 8 to 10 minutes. Consistency should be like fudge. Store in a jar in the fridge; freeze if keeping more than a few days.

Beef Cookies

Following the recipe for Liver Cookies, using cooked beef puree instead.

Mackerel Dinner

1 tsp. corn oil
1 ea. small mackerel
1/2 cup hot water

Heat corn oil in a skillet and fry mackerel until it flakes apart easily. Remove and cool. Pour the hot water into the pan and scrape the brown bits into it. Remove the bones from the fish and mix with the juice. For dogs, serve in pieces with kibble; for cats, grind with the pan juices.

Dog Morsels

2 cups whole wheat flour
2 tsp. garlic powder
2 cups white flour
1 cup skim milk powder
2 ea. eggs
1/2 cup melted beef or pork
drippings (or lard)
water

Preheat oven to 350 degrees. Mix all ingredients together with enough water to make a stiff dough. Roll out and cut into Christmas shapes. Bake on cookie sheet until hard.

Kitty Treats

1 1/2 cup rolled oats
1/4 cup vegetable oil, chicken broth or beef bouillon
1/2 cup flour

Preheat oven to 350 degrees.
Mix all ingredients into a dough.
Dust hands with flour and form
small, 1/2-inch-thick, round
"biscuits". Set on greased cookie
sheet. Bake 30 minutes (or until
biscuits are slightly browned).
Cool 30 minutes before serving.

Potatoes Au Canine or Feline

Serving Size: 6

3 cups boiled sliced potatoes
2 tbsp. grated vegetables
1/2 cup creamed cottage cheese
1 tbsp. nutritional yeast
2 tbsp. grated carrots
1/4 cup whole milk
1/4 cup grated cheese

Layer first 5 ingredients in a casserole dish. Then pour the milk on top of all; sprinkle with cheese. Bake about 15 minutes at 350 until cheese melts and slightly browns. Serve cool. As a potato substitute, you can use 3 cups of cooked oatmeal or 3 cups cooked brown rice.

Dog Cookies - Bread Maker

Bread Maker
Yield: 30 Cookies

1 cup beef, chicken or vegetable stock
1 cup bread OR all-purpose flour
1 cup Bulgar wheat
1 cup whole wheat or rye flour or other dark flour
1/4 cup non-fat dry milk powder
1 1/2 tsp. yeast

Use dough cycle. Roll dough to 1/4" thickness. Cut with cookie cutters or knife. Place on baking sheets sprinkled with cornmeal. Cover with clean kitchen towels and let rise in warm place about 45 minutes . Bake at 325-degrees for 45 minutes. When all are baked, turn off oven and return all cookies to cooling oven overnight to harden. Store in airtight container. [Using a 3.5" bone shaped cutter, I get about 30-35 cookies from this recipe. Cleo the Wonder Dog adores them].

(Machine) Dog Cookies

Dog Biscuit

1 cup beef, chicken, or vegetable stock
1 cup bread or all-purpose flour
1 cup whole wheat or rye (or other dark) flour
1 cup Bulgar wheat
1/4 cup non-fat dry milk powder
1/2 tsp. salt
1 1/2 tsp. yeast

Use dough cycle. Roll dough to 1/4" thickness. Cut with cookie cutters or knife. Place on baking sheets sprinkled with cornmeal. Cover with clean kitchen towels and let rise in warm place about 45 minutes. Bake at 325-degrees for 45 minutes. When all are baked, turn off oven and return all cookies to cooling oven overnight to harden. Store in airtight container.

(Using a 3.5" bone shaped cutter, I get about 30-35 cookies from this recipe. The Wonder Dog adores them.)

Microwave Easy Treat for Dogs

Yield: 1 Servings

3 jars meat or vegetable baby food
1/2 cup Cream of wheat

Mix together and drop by teaspoon on wax paper covered paper plate, flatten with a fork and cover with second plate. Microwave on HIGH for 2-5 minutes. Cool and store in refrigerator.

Notes: Microwave power wattage's may vary. 3 minutes for my microwave...

Puppy Treats

Yield: 10 servings
2 1/2 cups flour
1/2 cup powdered milk
1 tsp. garlic powder
2 tsp. onion powder
2 tsp. brown sugar

1 tsp. granulated bouillon
(fish)
6 tbsp. meat droppings
1 egg beaten
ice water

My dogs prefer fish flavored granulated bouillon, but you can use any flavor you wish. Combine it and the rest of the dry ingredients. Cut in drippings until mixture resembles cornmeal. Mix in egg. Add just enough water to make mixture form a ball. Pat (or roll) dough to 1/2" thick and cut into desired shapes. Small dogs (like mine) like bite sized pieces like stars about the size of a quarter. The general rule is the bigger the dog, the bigger the "cookie". The "10 servings" are for 6" bones. Place on a lightly greased cookie sheet. Bake at 350°, 25 to 30 minutes, until hard and dry. Cool before serving.

Midnight Stars To Go

Dogs love peanut butter! These high protein biscuits are terrific for any dog on the go. As an extra special treat, make a sandwich COOKIE by spreading some peanut butter and a drop of honey between two biscuits.

3 cups whole wheat flour	1 1/2 cup milk
1/2 cup rolled oats	1 1/2 cup peanut butter
2 tsp. baking powder	1/4 tbsp. molasses

Preheat the oven to 350 degrees.

Combine the flour, oats and baking powder in a large bowl. Using a food processor or blender, mix the milk, peanut butter and molasses until smooth and add to dry ingredients. Using your hands, knead the ingredients together. Dough will be quite stiff.

Roll the dough out to 1/4" thickness and cut with cookie cutters. Bake for about 20 minutes or until lightly browned. Turn off the heat and leave the biscuits in the oven until cool. Store in airtight container.

Nino's Passion Patties

These honey-flavored hearts are the perfect love substitute for the animal in your animal.

1 1/2 cup barley flour
1/2 cup soy flour
2 tsp. baking powder
1/2 cup dried currants

1/3 cup milk
1 tbsp. honey
3 tbsp. safflower oil

Preheat oven to 300 degrees.

Combine the flours, baking powder and currants in a medium-sized bowl. Stir in the milk, honey and oil.
Mix well.

On a floured board, roll the dough out to 1/4" thickness and cut with a heart-shaped cookie cutter. Bake on a lightly greased cookie sheet for about 20 minutes until lightly browned. Turn the heat off and leave the cookies in the oven until cool. Store in an airtight container in the refrigerator.

Jamaican Peanut Butter Balls

Our dog loves ice cubes, frozen peas, and frozen bananas. These little "Popsicle's" are easy to make and have been a hit with all our pup "tasters."

1 ea. ripe bananas
1 cup wheat germ
3/4 cup peanut butter

In a small bowl, mash banana and peanut butter together using a fork. Mix in wheat germ. Place in refrigerator for about an hour until firm.

With your hands, roll rounded teaspoonfuls of mixture into balls. Place on cookie sheet in freezer. When completely frozen, pack into airtight containers and store in freezer.

Garlic Biscuits

Yield: Makes about 7 dozen cookie size biscuits.

3 1/2 cups All-purpose flour
2 cups Whole wheat flour
2 cups Bran
1 cup Rye flour
1 cup Grits or cornmeal
1/2 cup Nonfat dry milk

1 tbsp. Dehydrated minced or powdered garlic
1 pk. dry yeast
1/4 cup warm water
2 cups Tomato juice (salt free suggested)

These are excellent nutritious treats for your family dog and won't hurt small kids in the family if they happen to eat one. Combine all dry ingredients. Dissolve yeast in warm water and add tomato juice. Mix with dry ingredients. Dough should be very stiff. Knead dough for about 3 minutes. Roll out on homed board to 1/4 to 1/2 inch thickness. Cut to desired size with knife or cookie cutters. Place on ungreased cookie sheet and bake at 300 degrees for 1 hour. Turn off oven. Leave biscuits overnight or at least 4 hours to harden.

Spoil-Em Sticks For Naughty Pups

This treat might seem a bit extravagant but isn't your pooch
worth it? Rich and chewy, this jerky is
guaranteed to bring out the best in
any dog.

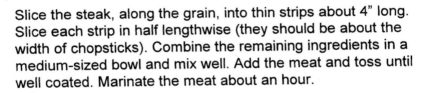

flank steak (about 2 pounds)
1/4 cup soy sauce
2 tsp. honey
1/4 tsp. garlic powder
1/4 tsp. onion powder

Preheat the oven to 150 degrees or
lowest setting.

Slice the steak, along the grain, into thin strips about 4" long.
Slice each strip in half lengthwise (they should be about the
width of chopsticks). Combine the remaining ingredients in a
medium-sized bowl and mix well. Add the meat and toss until
well coated. Marinate the meat about an hour.

Cover two cookie sheets with aluminum foil and place the
meat strips in a single layer without touching. Bake for about
7 hours until the meat is dry like jerky and dark in color. Store
in an airtight container in the refrigerator or freeze for longer
storage.

Healthy Eyes Appetizers

1/2 lb. ground beef
1 small carrot, finely grated
1 tbsp. grated cheese
1/2 tsp. garlic powder

1/2 cup whole wheat bread crumbs
2 eggs, beaten
1 tbsp. tomato paste

Preheat oven to 350 degrees.

In a medium-sized bowl, combine ground beef, carrot, cheese, garlic powder and bread crumbs. Add the egg and tomato paste and mix well. Using your hands, roll the mixture into marble-sized meatballs and place on a lightly greased cookie sheet. Bake for about 15 minutes until the meatballs are brown and firm. Cool the meatballs completely before storing in an airtight container in the refrigerator. These also freeze well.

Ground turkey works just as well as ground beef. The size of the meatballs can be varied according to the size of your dog. Serve these at room temperature or slightly warmed in the microwave.

Bowser's Breakfast Bagels

Unlike the human variety, these little canine bagels are crunchy. To soften them, for the occasional treat of bagels with cream cheese or peanut butter, stick them in the microwave for about 30 seconds.

1 cup whole wheat flour or other whole grain flour
1 cup unbleached white flour
1 pkg. yeast (1/4 ounce)

2/3 cup chicken stock, warmed
1 tbsp. honey
1/4 tsp. garlic

Preheat the oven to 375 degrees.

In a large bowl combine the whole wheat flour with the yeast. Add the chicken stock and honey and beat for about 3 minutes. Gradually add the remaining flour. Knead the dough for a few minutes until smooth. Cover the dough and let it rest for about 5 minutes. Divide the dough into about 25 pieces, rolling each piece into a smooth ball. Punch a hole into each ball with your finger and gently pull the dough so the hole is about an inch wide. Don't be too fussy here, the little bagels rise into shape when they bake. Place all the bagels on a greased cookie sheet and allow to rise for 5 minutes. Bake for 20 minutes. Turn the heat off and allow the bagels to cool in the oven.

Veggie Bites

2 eggs, beaten
1 cup grated cheese
1 cup cooked rice or bulgar
1 cup cooked vegetables, chopped, grated or mashed
(carrots, potatoes, zucchini, peas, etc.)
2 tbsp. chopped parsley, optional
1 tbsp. brewer's yeast

Preheat the oven to 350 degrees.

Mix all ingredients well. Drop by teaspoonful onto a greased cookie sheet. Bake for about 12 minutes or until set and lightly browned. Cool and store in an airtight container in the refrigerator. These bite-sized cheesy goodies will make any dog's mouth water. It's also a great recipe for using up leftovers!

Rebbeca's Barbecue Biscuit

These hardy biscuits can be sized for any dog. Just be sure to adjust the baking time accordingly.

2 cups whole wheat flour
1/2 cup bulgar (cracked wheat)
2 tbsp. brewer's yeast
2 cloves garlic, minced
1/4 cup vegetable oil

3/4 cup beef stock
1 beaten egg
2 tbsp. Worcestershire sauce
1 tbsp. catsup

Preheat the oven to 350 degrees.

Combine in a large bowl the flour, bulgar, brewer's yeast and garlic. Add oil and stock and mix well. The dough should be quite stiff. Add water if dough is too dry.

In a small bowl beat together the egg, Worcestershire sauce and the catsup.

Roll out to 1/9" thickness, depending on the size of your dog. Cut into appropriate-sized biscuits and brush with egg mixture. Bake on ungreased cookie sheet for about 35 minutes. Turn heat off and let biscuits dry out in oven for several hours.

Fish Cookies

Follow the recipe for Liver Cookies but use instead 3 1/2 ounces of mashed and boned tuna/white fish, either canned or freshly cooked.

Echo's Dog Biscuits-
Liver Flavored

1 1/2 cup flour
1 1/2 cup whole wheat flour
1 cup rye flour
1 cup oats
1 cup cornmeal

1/4 cup liver powder-(health food stores)
1 tsp. garlic powder
1 egg
1/2 cup vegetable oil
1 3/4 cup beef broth

Preheat oven to 300 degrees.
Place oven rack in upper third of oven. Line a cookie sheet with foil. Mix flours and all other dry ingredients in a large bowl. Add egg, oil, and beef broth. Mix the dough, adding enough additional flour to make a dough that can be rolled. On a floured surface, roll to 1/2 inch thickness, then cut into bone shapes with floured bone cookie cutter. Bake for 2 hours. Let biscuits stand in oven overnight to harden. Can be stored in plastic bags at room temperature for up to 1 month.

Echo's Liver Snacks

2 1/4 cup whole wheat flour
1 egg
1/2 cup vegetable oil
1 tbsp. brown sugar
1/2 cup nonfat dry milk

1/4 cup liver powder-(health food stores)
1 beef bouillon cube dissolved in 1/2 cup hot water
1 tbsp. garlic powder

Preheat oven to 300 degrees.
Mix all ingredients well. Knead for 2 minutes. Roll to 1/4 thick and cut with cutters of desired shapes. Bake on an ungreased cookie sheet for 30 minutes. Cool on rack.

Meaty Dog Biscuits

2 eggs
1/2 cup milk
2 cups beef or chicken broth
1 tsp. garlic powder
1 tbsp. yeast

3 1/2 cups all-purpose flour
2 cups whole wheat flour
1 cup rye flour
2 cups cracked wheat
1 tbsp. gravy master

Preheat oven to 325 degrees.
Mix all dry ingredients together. Stir in broth, gravy master, milk and eggs. Knead the mixture until dough forms, then roll out to 1/2 inch thickness. Cut into 1/2 inch squares. Place pieces on a cookie sheet and bake for 45 minutes. Leave biscuits in oven for 8 hours. Remove from oven and cool well before storing them.

Oscar Bones

1/3 cup margarine, softened
1/2 cup powdered milk
1 egg, beaten

3/4 cup hot water or meat juices
3 cups whole wheat flour

Preheat oven to 325 degrees.
In a large bowl pour hot water over margarine. Stir in powdered milk and egg. Add flour, 1/2 cup at a time mixing well after each addition. Knead 3 to 4 minutes, adding more flour if necessary to make a very stiff dough. Pat or roll to 1/2 inch thickness and cut out with a biscuit cutter. Place on a greased baking sheet and bake for 50 minutes. Allow to cool and dry out until hard.

Oreo's Cookie Treats

1 cup wheat germ
2 jars meat baby food

Preheat oven to 350 degrees.
Mix both together until you have a stiff dough. Form into balls
and place on cookie sheet. Flatten with fork. Bake in the oven
for 20-35 minutes until desired hardness. Can be frozen.

Hobbs Nutty Biscuits

1 3/4 cup flour
1/2 cup brown sugar
1 tsp. garlic powder
1 egg yolk
2 tbsp. toasted wheat
germ

1/4 cup sesame seeds
1/2 tbsp. butter
1/2 cup ground walnuts
1/2 cup vanilla extract

Preheat oven to 375 degrees.
Combine all ingredients, knead until thoroughly blended.
Divide dough into 6 parts, roll out each part into a log. Freeze.
When needed, thaw and roll into 1/2 thick slabs and cut into
bone shapes. Bake in the oven on an ungreased cookie
sheet for 13 minutes.

Chad's Molasses Almond Cookies

3 cups whole wheat flour
1/4 cup wheat germ
1/2 cup molasses
4 tbsp. margarine, softened
1 tsp. garlic
1/4 cup sliced almonds
1 egg, beaten

Preheat oven to 375 degrees.
Combine flour, wheat germ, garlic and almonds, cut into margarine, stir in egg, and molasses. Roll into ball, add water if needed. Roll on floured surface to 1/2" thick, cut into shapes and place on greased baking sheet and bake for 20 minutes.

Bobby's Peanut Butter Treats

3 cups whole wheat flour
1/2 cup rolled oats
2 tsp. baking powder
1 tsp. garlic powder

pinch of ginger powder
1 1/2 cups milk
1 1/4 cups peanut butter
1 tbsp. molasses

Preheat oven to 350 degrees.
Combine flour, oats and baking powder in a large bowl. Mix the milk, peanut butter and molasses until smooth, add dry ingredients. Knead the dough with hands, it will be stiff. Roll out to 1/4" thick and cut into shapes. Bake for 20 minutes or until lightly browned. Leave in oven to cool. Store in airtight container.

Perry's Dog Biscuits-
With Variations

2 1/2 cups whole wheat flour
1/2 cup nonfat dry milk
1 tsp. sugar
6 tbsp. margarine
1 egg
1 tsp. powdered beef
bouillon

Preheat oven to 350
degrees.
Mix ingredients with about 1/2 cup of cold water. Knead for 3
minutes. Dough should form a ball. Roll to 1/2" thick and cut
with dog bone cutters (or whatever you prefer). Bake on
lightly greased cookie sheet for 30 minutes. You could also
add powdered chicken bouillon or dried soup greens.

TJ's
Liver Brownies

1 lb. beef liver
1 cup corn meal
1 1/2 cup wheat flour
1 tsp. garlic powder
1 tsp. powdered beef bouillon
*NOTE - ham or turkey can be substituted for liver.

Preheat oven to 350 degrees.
Puree liver in food processor or blender, pour into bowl,
mixing in dry ingredients, adding flour a bit at a time until you
have a stiff mixture. Spread out on greased cookie sheet and
bake for 20 minutes or until dry. Cool and cut into squares.
Refrigerate or freeze.

Robbin's Biscuits

1 cup whole wheat flour
1/2 cup grated cheese
1/2 cup cooked peas or
carrots

1/4 lb. margarine
1 tsp. garlic powder
pinch of ginger

Preheat oven to 300 degrees.
Mix room temperature cheese and margarine together,
adding peas/carrots, garlic, ginger and flour. Add enough milk
to help form into a ball. Chill 1 hour, roll onto floured surface
and cut into shapes. Bake for 15 minutes or until slightly
brown.

Creamer's Refrigerated
Bran Muffins

2 1/2 cups all-purpose flour
2 1/2 tsp. baking soda
3 cups whole bran cereal
1 cup boiling water
2 eggs, beaten

2 cups buttermilk
1 1/2 cups sugar
1/2 cup cooking oil
1 cup raisins

Preheat oven to 400 degrees.
In mixing bowl stir together flour and baking soda. Set flour
mixture aside. In a small mixing bowl place 1 cup of the bran
cereal. Pour the boiling water over the cereal and set aside.
In large mixing bowl combine the eggs, buttermilk, sugar,
cooking oil, and remaining bran cereal. Add flour mixture to
egg mixture. Stir just until moistened then add the soaked
bran and stir just until well combined. Fold in raisins. Transfer
the batter to a covered container and refrigerate it overnight
or for up to 3 days. To Bake: Grease 2 1/2-inch muffin tins or
line muffin tins with paper baking cups. Spoon batter into the
prepared cups, filling each 2/3 full. Bake for 15-20 minutes or
until tops spring back when lightly touched.

Lamb's Dog Biscuits

2 1/2 cups all-purpose flour
1/2 cup vegetable oil
2 veg. bouillon cubes dissolved in 3/4 cup boiling water
3/4 cup dry milk
2 tbsp. brown sugar
1 egg
1/2 cup carrots
1/4 cup shredded celery

Preheat oven to 300 degrees.
Mix everything into a workable dough and roll out to about
1/4" thick. Cut with bone-shaped cookie cutter - or into strips -
or use cutter shape of your choice. Place on ungreased
cookie sheet and bake for 30 minutes.

Jack's
Carrot-Granola Muffins

1 1/4 cups all-purpose flour
2 tsp. baking powder
1/2 tsp. baking soda
1/2 tsp. ground allspice
1 1/2 cups low-fat granola
cereal
1/4 cup firmly packed
brown sugar
1 cup low-fat buttermilk
2 egg whites
2 tbsp. olive oil
1 cup grated carrots

Preheat oven to 400 degrees.
Spray 12 (2 1/2") muffin cups with vegetable cooking spray.
Stir flour, baking powder, baking soda and allspice until
blended. Set aside. Mix cereal, brown sugar and buttermilk in
a large bowl. Let stand for 5 minutes for granola to soften.
Stir in egg whites, oil and carrots. Stir in flour mixture until
blended. Spoon batter evenly to top of prepared muffin cups.
Bake for 20 minutes or until lightly browned.

Please Ma'
Turkey Meat Loaf

2 lbs. ground turkey
1 env. Lipton onion soup mix
1/4 cup ketchup
1 cup dry dog food
4 oz. mozzarella cheese, grated

Preheat oven to 350 degrees.
Mix all ingredients together. Spray 9 x 13-inch pan with a non-stick cooking spray. Divide the meat loaf mixture in half. Place half the mixture in the pan making a 9 x 5-inch rectangle. Put grated cheese on top of the meat loaf mixture. Place the remaining mixture on top of cheese sealing the edges. Spread top with ketchup and bake for 45 minutes or until done.

Garlic Oatmeal Cake

1/2 cup butter (margarine)
1 cup quick oatmeal
1 1/2 cup boiling water
2 eggs
1 1/2 cup flour

1 tsp. baking soda
1 tbsp. garlic powder
1 tsp. cinnamon
1/2 tsp. ginger
1/2 tsp. cloves

Preheat oven to 350 degrees.
Put butter and oatmeal in mixing bowl and pour water over this and let stand for 20 minutes. Add remaining ingredients and mix by hand. Pour into 9 x 13-inch pan, greased. Bake in oven for 30-35 minutes.

Scooby Snacks

1/2 cup powdered milk
1 egg, beaten
2 1/2 cups flour of choice
pinch of ginger
1/2 tsp. onion or garlic powder
1/2 cup cold water
6 tbs. meat drippings or margarine

Preheat oven to 350 degrees.
Mix, forming into a ball. Roll out to 1/2" thick, cut into shapes, re-roll scraps and repeat. Bake in oven for 25-30 minutes.

My Puppy Corn Patties

2 cups cornmeal
3 tbs. corn oil
pinch of garlic powder
1 cup water

Preheat oven to 375 degrees.
Place cornmeal, oil and salt in a bowl. In a saucepan, bring water to a boil over high heat and pour over cornmeal mixture, stirring well. Allow mixture to cool 10 minutes. Form mush into 2" patties with your hands. It helps to moisten your hands with oil or water. Place bones on prepared baking sheet and bake for 30 minutes or until firm.

Hen House Delight

8 oz. boiled chicken livers
1/2 cup cornmeal
1 cup wheat flour
1 tsp. garlic powder
1 tsp. beef bouillon

1 egg
1 tbsp. yeast flakes
2 tbsp. vegetable oil
Parmesan cheese

Preheat oven to 350 degrees.
Blend all in a food processor. Press into big cookie sheet about 1" thick, sprinkle parmesan cheese on top. Bake for 45 minutes, then cut into bite size squares, put back in oven at 200 degrees for 1 hour. Refrigerate in airtight container.

Sunday Brunch

1/2 lb. ground beef
1 carrot, finely grated
1 tsp. grated cheese
1/2 tsp. garlic powder
1/2 cup whole wheat bread crumbs
1 egg, beaten
1 tsp. tomato paste

Preheat oven to 350 degrees.
Combine all ingredients, mix well. Roll into meat balls. Place on greased cookie sheet. Bake 15 minutes or until brown and firm. Cool and store in fridge in airtight container or freeze.

Pet Party Mix

2 cups Cheerios®
2 cups spoon size Shredded Wheat®
2 cups Crispix®
1/2 cup melted butter
2 tbsp. garlic powder
2 tbsp. dry gravy mix
1/2 cup Kraft® grated American cheese powder
1/2 cup bacon bits
1 cup dog jerky/pupperoni/sausages

Preheat oven to 250 degrees.
Pour melted butter into 13 x 9 baking pan. Stir in cheese powder, bacon bits, garlic powder and gravy mix. Add cereals and stir well until all pieces are coated. Heat in oven for 45 minutes. Meanwhile, cut doggie meat treats into 1/2" pieces. Remove cereal from oven, add doggie treats. Store in airtight containers. May be frozen.

Monday's Snack

2 cups whole wheat flour
1/2 cup cornmeal
2/3 cup water
1 tsp. garlic
6 tbsp. oil

Preheat oven to 350 degrees.
Mix all ingredients. Roll out to 1/4" thick and cut into desired shapes. Bake for 35-40 minutes. Remove to wire rack and let cool thoroughly. Store in airtight container.

K-9 Chicken Taco Salad

2 whole chicken breasts, skinned and boned
1 tablespoon vegetable oil
1/2 cup plain yogurt
1 ripe avocado, peeled and mashed
1 teaspoon garlic powder
3 cups tortilla chips - crushed
3 cups shredded lettuce
1 can (15 ounces) kidney beans, drained and rinsed

1 large fresh tomato, chopped
Shredded cheese (cheddar, Monterey Jack, etc.)

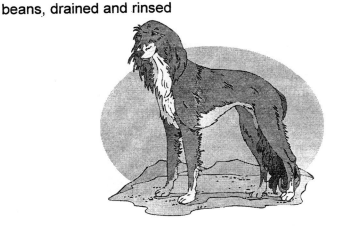

Cut the chicken breasts into cubes. Heat the oil in a large skillet; add the chicken and stir-fry over medium heat until no longer pink, 3-5 minutes. In a small bowl, blend together the avocado and garlic. To serve, arrange 1/4 of the tortilla chips on each serving plate; top with 1/4 of the lettuce, 1/4 of the beans, 1/4 of the chicken, and 1/4 of the tomato. Top each serving with a dollop of the yogurt mixture. Sprinkle with the cheese.

Pamper & Please Chicken Chowder

1 medium onion, chopped
1/4 cup chopped green
pepper
3 medium potatoes, peeled
and diced
2 medium carrots, sliced
1 large stalk celery, chopped
1-1/2 cups chicken broth -
low in salt

1-1/2 cups diced, cooked
chicken
1 can (17 ounces) cream-
style corn
1/2 teaspoon thyme
1/4 teaspoon garlic
3 cups milk

Place the onion, green pepper, potatoes, carrots, celery and
chicken broth in a large saucepan. Bring to a boil; reduce the
heat and simmer, covered, until the potatoes and carrots are
tender, about 10 minutes. Stir in the chicken, corn, thyme,
garlic and milk. Stirring occasionally, heat thoroughly but do
not boil. Serves 6. Mix with dry dog food - let stand for 10
minutes, then serve.

Black Lab's Spoonbread

1-1/2 cups boiling water
1 cup cornmeal
2 tablespoons butter or margarine

1/2 teaspoon garlic powder
3 eggs
1-1/2 cups milk

Pour the boiling water over the cornmeal in a large bowl; stir constantly until thick and smooth. Stir in the butter and garlic powder. Cool to lukewarm. In a separate bowl, beat together the eggs and milk. Add to the cornmeal mixture and mix until well blended. Pour into a greased 1-1/2 quart casserole dish. Bake in a preheated 375°F oven until golden brown, 35-45 minutes. The center will be soft, the edges crusty. Spoon out to serve while hot. Serves 6. Served hot from the oven.

Peanut Butter Love Cookies

3/4 cup butter or margarine
3/4 cup white sugar
3/4 cup brown sugar
2 eggs
1/2 teaspoon garlic

1 teaspoon vanilla extract
1 cup peanut butter
2 cups all-purpose flour
2 teaspoons baking soda

In a large bowl, cream together the butter or margarine, garlic, white sugar, and brown sugar. Add the eggs and vanilla; beat well. Blend in the peanut butter. In a separate bowl, combine the flour and baking soda. Gradually add to the creamed mixture; mix well. Drop by the tablespoon, about 2 inches apart, onto ungreased cookie sheets; press flat with a fork, making a criss-cross pattern. Bake in a preheated 350°F oven for 10-12 minutes. Remove the cookies to wire racks; cool. Makes about 60 cookies.

Pumpkin's Cornbread

1 cup cornmeal
1 cup all-purpose flour
1 tablespoon baking powder
1 teaspoon cinnamon
1/2 teaspoon nutmeg

2 eggs
1/2 cup vegetable oil
1 cup pumpkin puree
3/4 cup brown sugar
1/2 cup chopped bacon

In a large bowl, combine the cornmeal, flour, baking powder, cinnamon, and nutmeg. In a separate bowl, beat together the eggs, oil, pumpkin, and sugar until well mixed. Add to the flour mixture; stir until just moist. Stir in the bacon. Turn into a greased 9-inch square pan. Bake in a preheated 375°F oven until the surface springs back when lightly pressed, 30-40 minutes. Remove to a wire rack; serve warm. Makes 1 square loaf.

Wonder Dog's Oatmeal Drop Biscuits

1-1/4 cups all-purpose flour
1 tablespoon baking powder
1/4 cup butter or margarine
1 cup rolled oats
1 egg, beaten

1/3 cup milk
1/2 teaspoon garlic powder
2 tablespoons honey or
unsulphured molasses

In a large bowl, combine the flour and baking powder. Using a pastry blender or fork, cut in the butter until crumbly. Add the oats, egg, milk, and honey; stir until just moist. Drop the dough by well-rounded tablespoonfuls onto a greased baking sheet. Bake in a preheated 400°F oven for 8-10 minutes. Serve warm. Makes about 12 biscuits. Sprinkle with garlic powder.

Diamond's Bran Muffins

1 cup shredded bran cereal
(All Bran®, etc.)
1 cup milk
1 egg
1/4 cup vegetable oil
1-1/4 cups all-purpose flour
1/4 cup brown sugar
1 teaspoon garlic powder
1 tablespoon baking powder

In a large bowl, combine the cereal, milk, and garlic powder; let stand until the cereal is softened, about 5 minutes. Beat in the egg and oil. In a separate bowl, combine the flour, sugar, and baking powder. Add to the cereal mixture; stir until just moist. Fill greased muffin cups about 2/3 full with the batter. Bake in a preheated 400°F oven for 20-25 minutes. Cool on a wire rack for 10 minutes; remove from the pan. Makes 12 muffins.

<u>Variations</u>: Gently fold any of the following ingredients into the batter: 1/2 cup chopped dried fruit (dates, figs, apricots, etc.); 1/2 cup roasted sunflower seeds; 1/3 cup peanut butter.

Cheesy Timmy's Bran Muffins

1-1/4 cups all-purpose flour
3/4 cup oat bran (or wheat bran)
1 tablespoon baking powder
1/4 cup grated Parmesan cheese

1 cup finely chopped onion
1/4 cup plus 1 tablespoon vegetable oil
1 egg
3/4 cup milk
1 teaspoon garlic powder

In a large bowl, combine the flour, oat bran, garlic powder, baking powder, and cheese. In a small skillet, sauté the onion in the 1 tablespoon of oil over medium heat until tender, about 5 minutes. Remove to a small bowl; beat in the remaining 1/4 cup oil, the egg, and milk. Add to the flour mixture; stir until just moist. Fill greased muffin cups about 2/3 full with the batter. Bake in a preheated 375°F oven for 18-20 minutes. Cool on a wire rack for 5 minutes; remove from the pan. Serve warm. Makes 12 muffins.

Bran Doo Doo's

2 teaspoons garlic
1 cup wheat bran
2/3 cup milk
1 egg
1 cup whole wheat flour

1 cup all-purpose flour
3 tablespoons sugar
1 tablespoon baking powder
1/3 cup butter or margarine

In a large bowl, combine the wheat bran and milk; let stand until the bran is softened, about 3 minutes. Beat in the egg. In a separate bowl, combine the whole wheat flour, garlic, all-purpose flour, sugar, and baking powder. Using a pastry blender or a fork, cut the butter into the flour mixture until crumbly. Add to the bran mixture; stir with a fork until well blended. (The dough will be sticky.) Turn out onto a lightly floured surface and knead gently a few times. Divide the dough in half. Place each half on a greased baking sheet. Bake at 350°F for 25 minutes or until golden brown.

Easy Corn Oat Muffins

1 teaspoon garlic powder
1/2 cup cornmeal
1/2 cup rolled oats
1 cup plain yogurt
1/4 cup milk
1 egg

1/4 cup butter or margarine, melted
1 cup all-purpose flour
1 tablespoon baking powder
1/3 cup brown sugar

In a large bowl, combine the cornmeal, oats, yogurt, and milk; mix well. Beat in the egg, garlic, and butter. In a separate bowl, combine the flour, baking powder, and sugar. Add to the oat mixture; stir until just moist. Fill greased muffin cups about 2/3 full with the batter. Bake in a preheated 400°F oven for 20-25 minutes. Cool on a wire rack for 5 minutes; remove from the pan. Makes 12 muffins. Stir in 1/2 cup well-drained corn kernels before baking if you like.

Cleo's Turkey Cookies

3/4 cup butter or margarine
1/3 cup brown sugar
1/4 cup honey
2 eggs
1 teaspoon vanilla extract
1/2 teaspoon baking soda

2 cups rolled oats
1 cup whole wheat flour
1 cup raisins
1 cup chopped turkey bacon
2 cups coarsely crushed bran flakes cereal

In a large bowl, cream together the butter, sugar, and honey. Beat in the eggs, vanilla, and baking soda. Add the oats and flour; mix well. Fold in the raisins and bacon. Gently fold in the cereal. Drop by the tablespoon, about 2 inches apart, onto greased baking sheets. Bake in a preheated 350°F oven until lightly browned, 15-20 minutes. Let the cookies stand on the sheets 10 minutes before removing to wire racks to cool completely.

Turkey Bacon Grits

4 cups water
1 cup hominy grits
2 eggs, beaten
1/2 cup brown sugar

1/2 cup chopped turkey bacon
2 tablespoons butter or margarine
1 teaspoon vanilla extract

Bring the water to a boil in a large saucepan; slowly stir in the grits. Return the mixture to a boil; reduce the heat and simmer, stirring occasionally, until thickened, 12-15 minutes. Remove from the heat; cover and let stand for 5 minutes. Stirring constantly, add the eggs, sugar, bacon, butter, and vanilla. Turn the mixture into a greased 2-quart casserole. Bake in a preheated 350°F oven until a knife inserted near the center comes out clean, 50-60 minutes. Serve warm or cold.

"Sniff Sniff" Chicken Fried Rice

1 tablespoon vegetable oil
12 ounces skinless, boneless chicken breast or turkey breast tenderloins, cut into cubes
3 cups cooked rice
2 eggs, beaten

3 tablespoons chopped green onions
1/2 cup bean sprouts
1/2 cup chopped celery
1/2 teaspoon garlic powder
1-1 1/2 tablespoons reduced-sodium soy sauce
1 teaspoon sugar

In a large skillet, heat the oil. Add the chicken and stir-fry over medium heat until no longer pink, 3-5 minutes. Add the rice and stir-fry until well mixed. Add the eggs, onions, sprouts, celery, garlic powder, soy sauce, and sugar, stirring constantly until well combined. Continue to stir-fry until heated through. Serve immediately. Serves 4. This speedy dish is a good choice after a busy day.

Punky's Broiled Kidneys

Preheat broiler. Remove most of fat from veal kidneys. Cut them cross-wise into slices. Place 3 to 4 inches from source of heat and broil them about 5 minutes. Turn and baste with melted butter. Broil about 5 minutes longer or until done. Add paprika to taste.

Toni's Liver Loaf

1 cup water
1 medium sized chopped onion
3 chopped ribs celery with leaves
1 lb. Liver: beef, lamb, or pork

2 slices of bacon
1 or 2 beaten eggs
1 cup cracker or dry bread crumbs
1 cup liquid: reserved liver stock, milk, tomato juice, etc.

Preheat oven to 350°F. Boil water, onions, and celery for 5 minutes. Prepare liver for cooking, slice, add and simmer for 2 minutes. Drain, reserving the liquid. Put liver and vegetables through a meat chopper with bacon. Add eggs, cracker/bread crumbs, and cup of liquid to mixture and blend well. Place the meat in the pan. Bake about 40 minutes.

Tanya's Boiled Fresh Beef Tongue

A fresh beef or calf tongue, about 2 lbs.
2 medium sized onions

2 large carrots
3 or more ribs celery with leaves

Barely cover these ingredients with boiling water. Skim off any fat after first 5 minutes. Simmer the tongue uncovered until tender (about 50 minutes per pound). Drain and reserve liquid. Skin and trim the tongue. Reheat in the cooking water before serving.

8-Ball's Marrow Balls

1/4 cup fresh marrow
2 tablespoons butter
3 egg yolks
1/8 teaspoon paprika

2 tablespoons chopped
parsley
cracker crumbs
3 stiffly beaten egg whites

Combine marrow and butter. Add yolks, paprika, parsley, and cracker crumbs. Use at least 1/2 cup of cracker crumbs to make the mixture of a stiff consistency to shape into balls with egg whites. Cook the balls in simmering water for 15 minutes or until they rise to the surface.

Shep's Ham Loaf

1 lb. smoked, cooked ham,
ground
1 lb. ground lean pork
2 eggs, lightly beaten
1/4 cup milk

1/2 cup cracker crumbs
3/4 cup light brown sugar
1/3 cup cider vinegar
1/3 cup water

Preheat the oven to 350°F. Combine the ham, pork, eggs, milk, cracker crumbs, and pack into a loaf pan. Bake for 45 minutes. Meanwhile, combine the remaining ingredients in a saucepan, bring to a boil and boil for 5 minutes. Bake the ham loaf 45 minutes longer, basting frequently with the sauce.

Rambo's Baked Marrow Bones

Preheat oven to 300 degrees. Saw into 2-inch pieces 2 lb. shin bone or knuckle of veal. Dip the bones first in olive oil then in seasoned flour. Brown the bones upright as close together as possible in a heavy pot just large enough to hold them. Cook until golden in the fat 1/4 cup chopped onions. Add them to the bones. Heat and pour over the bones 1/3 cup white wine and 1/2 cup of diced fresh tomatoes, seasoned stock -- enough to cover the lower third of the bones. Cover and bake for 1 to
1-1/2 hours until any meat on the bones is tender.

Blodgett's Parsnip Fritters

5 parsnips
1 tablespoon butter
1 teaspoon flour

1 egg, lightly beaten
bacon drippings or butter

Cook the parsnips in boiling salted water to cover. Drain, peel and mash. Beat in the butter, flour, and egg. Form the mixture into small, flat, round or oval cakes. Heat bacon drippings in a large heavy skillet so that there is about one-quarter-inch depth. Fry the cakes, a few at a time until golden brown, turn and brown the other side. Drain on paper towels and keep warm.

Brandy's Red Flannel Hash

2 cups chopped cooked
corned beef
3 cups diced cooked potatoes
1-1/2 cups diced cooked
beets

2 tablespoons grated onion
1 teaspoon Worcestershire
sauce
2 tablespoons bacon
drippings

In a bowl, combine the corned beef, potatoes, beets, onion, and Worcestershire sauce. Heat the bacon drippings in a heavy skillet and spread the corned beef mixture over bottom of skillet. Cook over medium-high heat until underside of hash is browned. Turn and brown the other side.

Jake's High Fiber Bread

2 cups flour
1/3 cup sugar
1 teaspoon baking soda
1-1/2 cups rolled oats
1 cup whole bran cereal

1/2 cup raisins
2 eggs, lightly beaten
1-1/3 cups buttermilk
1/2 cup light molasses

Preheat oven to 350 degrees. Sift together the flour, sugar, and baking soda. Stir in the oats, bran and raisins. Combine the eggs, buttermilk and molasses. Add to dry ingredients and stir until just moistened. Pour into a greased 9-by-5-by-3-inch loaf pan. Bake one hour, or until done.

Nick's Wild Rice Ring

1 cup wild rice
You may add:
1 pressed clove garlic
When rice is tender add:
1/4 cup butter
1/2 teaspoon poultry seasoning or freshly grated nutmeg
1 cup sautéed onions and mushrooms
1/4 cup dry sherry

Preheat oven to 350 degrees.
Place wild rice in a well-greased 7-inch ring mold set in a pan of hot water in the oven. Bake about 20 minutes. Loosen the edges with a knife, invert the contents onto a platter.

Poor Rose's Cookies

2 1/2 cups whole wheat flour
1/2 cup cornmeal
1/2 cup wheat germ
1/2 cup sweet and sour sauce
2 tablespoons brown sugar

1 tablespoon honey
2 tablespoons vegetable oil
2 eggs
1/2 cup water
pinch of garlic

Preheat oven to 350 degrees.
Combine dry ingredients. In a separate bowl, mix honey, oil, eggs, water and sweet and sour sauce. Add dry ingredients. Roll dough to 1/4" thick, cut with a cookie cutter, and place on an ungreased cookie sheet. Bake for 25-30 minutes until golden brown.

Fino's Chicken Lasagna

2 cups uncooked enriched elbow macaroni
1 cup cottage cheese
1 large carrot (shredded)
2 medium diced tomatoes
1/2 tsp. garlic powder
6 chicken thighs

Cook macaroni then cool. Boil chicken thighs, remove skin, debone, then chop meat. Save chicken broth and add shredded carrots, garlic, diced tomatoes, macaroni, and chicken. Last, add cottage cheese, then mix and serve.

Ritz Cookies

1 cup whole wheat flour
1/2 cup bran
1/2 cup brewers yeast
1/4 cup wheat germ
1/2 teaspoon cinnamon
2 tablespoons honey

2 teaspoons molasses
1 pinch garlic powder
2 tablespoons corn oil
2 eggs
1/3 cup milk

Preheat oven to 350 degrees.
In a large bowl combine all dry ingredients. In a separate bowl, beat honey, molasses, corn oil, egg, and milk. Gradually add mixture to dry ingredients to form a dough. Roll dough 1/4" thickness and cut into bone shapes. Bake on an ungreased cookie sheet for 17 minutes or until lightly golden brown.

Birthday Beef Stew

2 cups white rice (uncooked)
1 1/2 lb. hamburger
1 jar fat free beef gravy
1 large carrot (shredded)
2 cups water
pinch of garlic powder

Cook rice and hamburg then drain. Add shredded raw carrot and garlic. Add water and gravy. Mix and let cool.

Johnnycakes

1 cup white cornmeal
1 cup boiling water
1/3-1/2 cup milk

Place the cornmeal in a large bowl, stir in the boiling water. Mix well and let stand for ten minutes. Beat in enough milk to make a batter stiff enough to hold its shape on a spoon. Drop the batter by tablespoon into a lightly greased skillet. Cook over medium heat until golden and crisp around the edges. About 3 minutes on each side.

Gina's Breakfast Bran Muffins

1 1/4 cup shredded bran
cereal
1 cup orange juice
1 egg
1/4 cup all-purpose flour
2 teaspoons baking powder
1/2 teaspoon baking soda
1/4 cup beef broth

Preheat oven to 400 degrees.
In a large bowl, combine the cereal and juice. Let stand until
cereal is softened, about 5 minutes. Beat in the egg and oil.
In a separate bowl, combine the flour, baking powder, baking
soda, and beef broth. Add to the cereal mixture; stir until just
moist. Fill greased muffin cups about 2/3 full with the batter.
Bake in the oven 20-25 minutes. Cool on a wire rack for 5
minutes; remove from the pan.

Wag the Dog Muffins

1 cup whole wheat flour
1 cup all-purpose flour
2 teaspoons baking powder
1 teaspoon garlic powder
1/2 teaspoon baking soda
2 eggs, beaten

1/2 cup milk
1/4 cup vegetable oil
1/2 cup molasses
1 cup finely shredded carrots
1/2 cup chopped dates

Preheat oven to 400 degrees. In a large bowl, combine the whole wheat flour, all-purpose flour, baking powder, garlic powder, and baking soda. In a separate bowl, mix together eggs, milk, oil, and molasses; add to the flour mixture. Stir until just moist. Stir in the carrots and dates. Fill greased muffin cups 2/3 full with the batter. Bake in the oven for 20-25 minutes. Cool on a wire rack for 5 minutes; remove from pan. Pack these moist muffins for a hiking trip with your best friend.

Classy Simon's Peanut Butter Muffins

1/2 cup yellow cornmeal
1-1/2 cups all-purpose flour
1/4 cup brown sugar
1 tablespoon baking powder
1/2 cup peanut butter

1 cup milk
1 egg
3 tablespoons vegetable oil
1 teaspoon garlic powder

Preheat oven to 400 degrees. In a large bowl, combine the cornmeal, flour, garlic powder, brown sugar, and baking powder. In a separate bowl, mix the peanut butter and 1/2 cup milk until smooth. Beat in the egg, oil, and remaining 1/2 cup of milk. Add to the flour mixture; stir until just moist. Fill greased muffin cups about 2/3 full with the batter. Bake in the oven for 20-25 minutes. Cool on a wire rack for 5 minutes; remove from the pan.

Hanover Muffins

1 cup yellow cornmeal
1 cup all-purpose flour
2 tablespoons sugar
1 tablespoon baking powder
2 eggs
1 cup milk

1/4 cup butter or margarine
(melted)
1/2 cup chopped green
pepper
1/2 cup shredded carrot
1/2 cup finely chopped onion

Preheat oven to 400 degrees. In a large bowl, combine the
cornmeal, flour, sugar, and baking powder. In a separate
bowl, beat together the eggs, milk, and butter; add to the flour
mixture. Stir until just moist. Fold in the pepper, carrot, and
onion. Fill greased muffin cups about 2/3 full with the batter.
Bake in the oven for 20-25 minutes. Cool on a wire rack for 5
minutes; remove from pan.

Rusty's Peanut Butter Dog Bones

1 tablespoon vegetable oil
3/4 cup peanut butter
1 cup whole wheat flour

1 egg
1 cup water

Preheat oven to 350 degrees. In a large bowl combine oil,
egg, peanut butter, and water. Add flour, one cup at a time;
knead into a firm dough. Roll dough 1/4" thickness and cut
with dog bone cookie cutter. Place on cookie sheet and bake
for 25 minutes.

Metro's Cheese Logs

1-1/2 cups shredded cheddar cheese
1/2 cup margarine (softened)
1-1/2 cup whole wheat flour
pinch garlic powder
1/4 cup milk
1/4 cup shredded carrots

Preheat oven to 375 degrees. Cream together cheese, margarine, and carrots. Add flour, garlic, and milk. Roll into 1/4" thick log. About every 4", cut to make 2 dozen sticks. Bake for 20 minutes. You try one!

Spring Time Biscuits

3-1/2 cups wheat flour
1/2 cup cornmeal
1/2 cup diced celery
1/8 cup diced sweet onion
1/2 cup shredded carrot
1/2 cup unsalted sunflower seeds
1-1/4 cups water
pinch of garlic powder
3 tablespoons vegetable oil

Preheat oven to 350 degrees. In large bowl combine water and oil. Mix into flour, corn meal, vegetables, garlic and sunflower seeds. Knead dough for 4 minutes and roll to 1/4" thick. Use a cookie cutter to make 3 dozen. Place on ungreased cookie sheet and cook for 30 minutes until golden.

Salmon Pie

1 can salmon
2 cups rice (cooked)
2 cups dry dog food
2 cups water
1/2 teaspoon garlic powder

Preheat oven to 350 degrees. Mix all of the ingredients together into a casserole dish and bake for 10-12 minutes.

Breakfast of Champions

1 cup dry dog food
4 cups Special K® cereal
1 can chicken or beef broth
(salt-free)

1/2 cup fat free cottage
cheese
3 cups water
1 apple diced 1/4"
1 banana

Mix all above ingredients.

Sage and Rice Hamburger

1 pound hamburger
1 egg, slightly beaten
1/2 cup soft bread crumbs
4 tablespoons
1 medium-sized onion, cut into 1/4" pieces
1 clove garlic, sliced very thin
2 cups warm water with 3 beef bouillon cubes dissolved in it
2 cups precooked rice
1/2 teaspoon powdered sage
1/2 cup Parmesan-Romano cheese

Mix the hamburger with the slightly beaten egg and the bread crumbs. Form into 8 small patties about 2" in diameter. Melt the butter in a large skillet with a tight-fitting cover. Brown the meat patties on both sides in the butter. Remove the patties with a spatula and set in a warm place. Reserve the remaining butter.
Sauté the onion and garlic in the remaining butter until the onion is slightly transparent. Add the bouillon to the onion. Add the rice just as it comes from the package; then add the sage. Stir very well. Cook over low heat, tightly covered, for 10 minutes, or until all of the rice has doubled in size and is tender and separated.

Place the sage rice on a heated platter with the hamburger patties around the edge. Sprinkle the rice with the cheese. Place under the broiler for 3 or 4 minutes, or until the  cheese begins to brown. Serve cool with dry food.

Green Rice with Hamburger

2 tablespoons
1 pound hamburger
1 onion, chopped fine
2 cups water
2 cups instant rice
1 can strained baby food spinach
1 tablespoons parsley, chopped fine

Melt the butter in a skillet and brown the hamburger. Add the onion and continue to cook until onion is transparent.
Place the water in a saucepan and bring to a rapid boil. Stir in the rice. Cover tightly and cook for 5 minutes, or until all the kernels are separated. Then stir in the strained spinach. Add the hamburger and onion.

Quick Meat Sauce Over Rice

1 pound hamburger
2 tablespoons cornstarch
2 cups V-8® vegetable juice cocktail
1 beef bouillon cube
2 cups precooked rice
2 cups water

Brown the hamburger in a skillet until it loses its reddish color. Stir the cornstarch into the V-8® juice and pour over the rice in a large serving bowl, make a hollow in the center and pour in the thickened meat sauce.

Ten Variations for the Meat Sauce:

1. Stir in 2 cups dry dog food 5 minutes before serving.
2. Substitute 1 8-ounce package broad cooked noodles for the rice.
3. Add 2 packages frozen lima beans 5 minutes before serving.
4. Add 2 packages frozen peas with little onions 5 minutes before serving.
5. Omit the rice and stir into the meat sauce 1/2 can pork and beans.
6. Add 2 packages frozen zucchini squash 5 minutes before serving.
7. Add 2 packages frozen green beans 5 minutes before serving.
8. Add 1 small can mushroom stems and pieces, drained, 5 minutes before serving.
9. Add 1small can yellow butter beans 5 minutes before serving.

Omit the rice and add 2 small cans macaroni and cheese 5 minutes before serving.

Serbian Meat Balls

1/2 pound ground lamb
1/2 pound ground beef
1/2 teaspoon thyme
1/4 teaspoon garlic
1 tablespoon olive oil
3 eggs, separated
1 teaspoon yogurt
dash of garlic
dash of thyme
1 teaspoon paprika

Mix the lamb and beef together thoroughly. Season with the 1/2 teaspoon thyme and 1/4 teaspoon garlic and form into meat balls about the size of golf balls. Heat the olive oil in a deep skillet and brown the meat balls on all sides.
Meanwhile, beat the egg yolks until they are light and lemon colored. Stir the yogurt into the egg yolks, mixing very well. Add a dash of thyme, a dash of garlic and the paprika. Mix again. Beat the egg whites until they stand in peaks. Fold into the yogurt-egg yolk mixture.
Remove the meat balls from the skillet and place them in a deep baking dish. Pour over this the yogurt-egg mixture. Cook at 350° F. for about 20 minutes, or until the sauce is thickened.
Serve with dry dog food or plain boiled rice.

Chick Peas and Meat Balls

1 pound (approximately) soup bone
4 strips lean bacon, cut into 1/4" pieces
3 cups water
1 cup dried chick peas, soaked overnight in 3 cups water
1 stalk leek, cut into fine pieces
1 large carrot, cut into 1/8" slices
2 medium-sized raw potatoes, scrubbed but not peeled, diced in 1/2" pieces
1 pound hamburger
1 small green pepper, chopped very fine
1 small onion, chopped very fine
1/4 teaspoon pepper
2 eggs, beaten until they are lemon yellow

Place the soup bone and bacon in the water and bring to a rolling boil. Drain the soaked chick peas and add them. Skim the froth from time to time as it rises to the top. Boil for 1 hour, or until the chick peas are tender. Remove the soup bone and discard. Add the leek, carrot, and raw potatoes. Simmer for an additional 30 minutes.

Meanwhile, mix the hamburger, green pepper, onion, pepper and eggs very well. Form into meat balls about 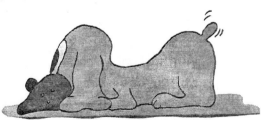 the size of golf balls and drop into the simmering chick pea mixture. Simmer for 30 minutes longer. Turn the mixture from time to time to keep it from sticking to the bottom of the pan and to insure even cooking of the meat balls.
Serve in a large tureen, garnished with dry dog food.

Seb's Milk-Rich Meat Loaf

If some man's best friends refuse to drink their quota of milk, this is a marvelous way to slip in an extra pint.

1/4 teaspoon paprika
1 egg
1 1/2 pounds ground veal, pork and beef (most supermarkets sell it packaged in equal portions of these three kinds of meat)
1/4 cup flour
2 cups scalded milk
1 small onion, grated, or 1/4 cup dehydrated onion, soaked in 1/4 cup milk
2 cups soft bread crumbs
1/2 teaspoon garlic powder
1/2 teaspoon ginger
1/8 teaspoon nutmeg
1/8 teaspoon cinnamon

A fluted type of mold is wonderful for this meat loaf; if you do not own one, a regular loaf tin will do. Butter all sides of the mold and sprinkle lightly with paprika. (Paprika gives a rich brown color to meat.) Beat the egg slightly and add to the meat mixture. Alternately add the flour and the scalded milk to the meat mixture. Add the onion, and work in the bread crumbs. Add the garlic, ginger, nutmeg and cinnamon. Stir all well to mix the flavors thoroughly. Turn into greased mold form or baking tin.

Place mold in a pan of hot water in a preheated 350° F. oven. Bake at 1 hour, or until the center of the loaf is firm to the touch. Turn out on a warmed platter. Garnish with parsley and rings of boiled carrots, if desired.

Wheaties Meat Loaf with Vegetable Soup

1 1/2 pounds hamburger
1/4 cup chopped onion
1/2 teaspoon garlic
1/2 teaspoon thyme
2 cups Wheaties® cereal
1 egg, beaten with 1 tablespoon water
1 can beef-vegetable soup

Mix all of the ingredients with the exception of the soup. Stir until all are well blended. Finally, fold in the soup, taking care that you do not mash the vegetables beyond identification. Put into a greased loaf pan and bake in a preheated 250° F. oven for 1 hour, or until center of loaf is firm to the touch. Baste from time to time with the liquid which gathers around the loaf.
This loaf is very colorful when sliced. It is excellent served cold.

Variations:

Substitute 1 can cream of mushroom soup for the beef-vegetable soup.
Substitute 1 can cream of chicken soup for the beef-vegetable soup.
Substitute 1 can cream of celery for beef vegetable soup.
For a wonderful flavor, add 3 tablespoons wheat germ.
Substitute Corn Flakes® for Wheaties®.
Substitute Cheerios® for Wheaties®.
Substitute 4 Shredded Wheat® biscuits for Wheaties®.
Substitute Rice Chex® for Wheaties®.

Tigger's Bones

1 cup uncooked oatmeal
1/4 cup margarine
1 1/2 cup hot water or meat juices
1/2 cup powdered milk
4 oz (1 cup) grated cheese such as cheddar, jack, swiss, colby or any other hard one
1/4 tablespoon garlic
1 egg, beaten
1 cup cornmeal
1 cup wheat germ
3 cups whole wheat flour

In a large bowl pour hot water over oatmeal and margarine: let stand for 5 minutes. Stir in powdered milk, grated cheese, garlic and egg. Add cornmeal and wheat germ. Mix well. Add flour, 1/3 cup at a time, mixing well after each addition. Knead 3 to 4 minutes, adding more flour if necessary to make a very stiff dough. Pat or roll dough to 1/2" thickness. Cut into bone shaped biscuits and place on a greased baking sheet. Bake for 1 hour at 300 degrees. Turn off heat and leave in oven for 1 1/2 hours or longer.

Happy New Years Cheese Biscuits

1 cup oats, rolled
1/3 cup butter
1 cup water
3/4 cup cornmeal
1 tablespoon sugar
1 teaspoon bouillon, beef
1/2 cup milk
4 oz cheese, cheddar, shredded
1 egg, beaten
3 cups flour, whole wheat

Boil water. Combine oats, butter and water. Let stand ten minutes. Stir in cornmeal, sugar, bouillon, milk, cheese and egg. Mix well. Add flour, a cup at a time, mixing well after each addition to form a stiff dough. On floured surface, knead in remaining flour until dough is smooth and no longer sticky, 3 to 4 minutes. Roll or pat out dough to 1/2" thickness. Cut with bone shaped cookie cutter. Place 1" apart on greased cookie sheets. Bake in preheated 325 degree oven 35 to 45 minutes or until golden brown. Cool completely.

Ginger's Cheddar Cheese Cookies

1/2 pound cheddar cheese, grated
1/4 pound margarine, softened
1 egg
1 clove garlic, minced
1 1/2 cups whole wheat flour
1/2 cup wheat germ
1/8 cup milk

Cream room temperature cheese and margarine. Add egg and garlic. Mix well. Add flour and wheat germ. Mix well until is forms a dough. Add milk and mix again. Chill 1 hour. Preheat oven to 375° F. Roll dough on floured surface to 1/4". Cut into shapes. Bake on ungreased cookie sheet 15 to 18 minutes.

Bambi's

2 cups all-purpose white flour
1 cup whole wheat flour
1 cup cornmeal
3/4 cup regular wheat germ
1/2 cup nonfat dry milk powder
2 teaspoons garlic powder
1 package active dry yeast
1/4 cup warm water
1 can (10 3/4 oz) beef broth
1 egg, slightly beaten
2 tablespoons milk

Combine the flours, cornmeal,
wheat germ, dry milk powder
and garlic powder in a very
large bowl. Activate the yeast in
the warm water and add it along with the beef broth to the dry
ingredients. Mix well with hands, for the dough will be very
stiff. Divide dough into halves and roll each half out on a
floured board to a thickness of 1/4". Cut into shapes with a
cookie cutter. Place fairly close together on an ungreased
baking sheet. Combine beaten egg and milk; brush over
surface of each cookie. Bake in a 300 degree oven for 45
minutes. Turn off the oven heat but leave baking sheet with
cookies in the oven to harden overnight. If you lack room in
the oven for all of them, then just place them in a dry spot
until they are quite hard.

Seazar's Favorite Treats Dog Biscuits

Yield: 1 batch
1 cup rolled oats
1/3 cup margarine
1 cup boiling water
3/4 cup cornmeal
1 tablespoon sugar
1 to 2 teaspoons chicken or beef flavored instant bouillon
1/2 cup milk
4 oz (1 cup) shredded cheddar cheese
1 each egg, beaten
2 cups to 3 cups all-purpose or whole wheat flour

Heat oven to 325 degrees. Grease cookie sheets. In a large
bowl, combine rolled oats, margarine and boiling water. Let
stand 10 minutes. Stir in cornmeal, sugar, bouillon, milk,
cheese and egg. Mix well. Lightly spoon flour into measuring
cup; level off. Add flour 1 cup at a time, mixing well after each
addition to form a stiff dough. On floured surface, knead in
remaining flour until dough is smooth and no longer sticky, 3
to 4 minutes. Roll or pat out dough to 1/2" thickness, cut with
bone shaped cookie cutter. Place 1" apart on greased cookie
sheets. Bake 325 degrees for 35 to 45 minutes or until golden
brown. Cool completely. Store loosely covered. Makes 3 1/2
dozen large dog biscuits or 8 dozen small dog biscuits.

Brian's Chicken Liver

2 cups flour
1 cup wheat germ
1/2 cup chicken broth
1 cup cooked, chopped chicken liver
3 tablespoons vegetable oil
1 egg, lightly beaten
2 teaspoons chopped parsley

Preheat oven to 400° F. Combine flour and cornmeal. In separate bowl, beat egg with oil, then add broth and parsley. Mix well. Add dry ingredients to bowl a little at a time, stirring well. Fold in chicken livers and mix well. Dough will be firm. Turn dough on lightly floured surface and knead briefly. Roll out 1/2" thick and cut into shapes. Place on greased cookie sheet 1" apart. Bake 15 minutes or until firm. Store in refrigerator.

Natural Chicken Biscuits

1 package dry yeast
1/4 cup warm water
1 pint chicken stock
3 1/2 cups unbleached flour
2 cups whole wheat flour
1 cup rye flour
2 cups cracked wheat or wheat germ
1/2 cup dry milk
1 egg
1 tablespoon milk

Beat egg with 1 tablespoon milk. Dissolve yeast in 1/4 cup warm water. Add to chicken stock. Combine all dry ingredients. Add chicken stock mixture. Knead on a floured surface for about 3 minutes, working into a stiff dough. Roll out to a thickness of 1/4". Cut into bars or with a cookie cutter. Brush with egg/milk wash and place on cookie sheets. Bake in 300 degree oven for about 45 minutes. Turn off heat and leave biscuits in oven overnight.

Eat-More Casserole

1 pound hamburger
1/2 pound elbow macaroni
1 cup chopped onion or 1/2 cup dehydrated onion soaked in
1/2 cup water
1 #2 can tomatoes
1 cup tomato sauce
1/4 teaspoon pepper
1/4 teaspoon garlic powder
1 teaspoon Accent®
1 cup dry dog food

Sauté the hamburger until a golden brown. Meanwhile, boil
the macaroni until tender. Drain the macaroni and combine it
with the hamburger; add the onion, tomatoes, tomato sauce,
pepper, garlic powder and Accent® to the meat. Last, fold in
the dog food.
Place this mixture in a 1 1/2-quart buttered casserole and put
into a preheated 350° F. oven; bake for 45 minutes.

White Fang's Hamburger Dumplings

6 strips bacon
1/2 pound hamburger
1 tablespoon dehydrated parsley
1 tablespoon chopped chives. or two scallions, cut very fine
1/4 teaspoon pepper
6 slices white bread soaked in 1 cup milk
3 eggs, beaten until lemon yellow
3 tablespoons butter
3/4 cup fine bread crumbs

Dice the bacon very fine and put into a skillet. Fry until it is golden brown and crisp. Remove the bacon from the pan with a slotted spoon and set aside. Now sauté the hamburger in the bacon fat until it is browned. Stir in the parsley, chives and pepper. Remove from heat. Set aside to cool.
Squeeze the milk from the bread and add the bread to the hamburger; now stir in the beaten eggs and mix very well. Form the mixture into small balls about the size of golf balls. Drop into rapidly boiling water and cook for about 12 minutes. Meanwhile, melt the butter and brown the bread crumbs in it. Place the dumplings on a heated platter; sprinkle the browned bread crumbs over the top. Decorate with the tiny pieces of crisp bacon.

Hamburger and Rice Casserole

1 pound hamburger
1 teaspoon onion juice or 1 tablespoon onion,
chopped very fine
1/2 cup celery, chopped fine
1/4 teaspoon ground black pepper
1 teaspoon garlic
Dash of nutmeg
1 8-ounce can tomato sauce
1 egg
2 cups cooked regular rice
1/2 cup dry dog food
1 tablespoon butter or margarine

Put the hamburger into a good-sized mixing bowl; add the
onion, celery, black pepper, garlic and nutmeg. Mix all very
thoroughly; then stir in the tomato sauce.
In another mixing bowl, beat the egg with a rotary beater until
light and lemon colored. Add the rice and mix thoroughly.
Press half the rice-egg mixture around the sides and over the
bottom of a well-greased casserole. Reserve the other half of
the rice to go over the top.
Place this casserole under the broiler for 5 minutes, or until
the rice begins to brown and is set firmly around the sides.
Remove from the oven, and put in the meat mixture carefully,
using a rubber spatula to spread it evenly. Cover with the
remainder of the rice-egg mixture, and sprinkle the dog food
over the top. Dot with the butter or margarine.
Bake at 350° F. for 45 minutes. Just before serving, place
under the broiler for a few seconds to brown the crumbs on
top.

You're My Honey

1/4 cup honey
1 egg, beaten
1/4 tablespoon garlic powder
2 cups all purpose flour
1 cup cornmeal
1 cup wheat germ
2 cups cracked wheat
4 cups whole wheat flour

In a small bowl, dissolve the yeast in warm water. In a large bowl, combine the broth, powdered milk, margarine, honey, egg and garlic. Add yeast/water and mix well. Stir in flour, cornmeal, wheat germ and cracked wheat. Mix well. Add whole wheat flour, 1/2 cup at a time, mixing well after each addition. Knead in the final amounts of flour by hand and continue kneading for 4 or 5 minutes until dough is not sticky. Pat or roll to 1/2 inch thickness and cut into bone shapes. Place on greased cookie sheet, cover lightly and let set for 20 minutes. Bake in a 350 degree oven for 45 minutes. Turn off heat and leave in the oven several hours or over night.

Summer Ice

2 fresh beef (or other species) marrow bones, each at least
1" thick
water
1 teaspoon garlic powder

In about a 2-quart pan, put the bones, add garlic and enough
water to cover the bones. Bring water to a boil; continue to
boil for at least 10 minutes. (More is okay, for a richer broth.)
Remove bones, and return any beef marrow to the liquid,
along with any meat that you can get off the bones. Cool the
broth to room temperature. Pour liquid only into 2-4 ice cube
trays. Chop up the marrow/meat/gristle into little bits, and put
them into each section of the tray. Freeze solid. Serve 2-3
cubes to your Beardie on a very hot day. (Not too many if you
made the broth very rich with extra bones or lots of marrow.)

Keystone Dog Treats

1/2 cup cornmeal
6 tablespoons oil
2/3 cup water or meat broth
2 cups whole wheat flour
1 teaspoon garlic powder

Mix ingredients well. Roll out to 1/4" thick. Cut into shapes
with cutter. Baste with meat drippings. Bake at 350 degrees F
for 35-40 minutes.

Pig's Feet Biscuits

5 cups whole wheat flour
1 cup milk
2 eggs
10 tablespoons vegetable oil or bacon fat

1 pinch onion or garlic powder
1/2 cup cold water
1 tablespoon vegetable oil or bacon fat

Mix all ingredients well. Pinch off pieces of the dough and roll them into two-inch balls. Put them on a greased cookie sheet. Bake them at 350 degrees for 35-40 minutes. Let them cool, then store in an airtight container.

I Love You! Cookies

2 cups whole wheat flour
2 cups Soya flour
1 cup wheat germ
1 cup cornmeal
1 cup nonfat dry milk

1 cup nutritional yeast flakes (from Health Food Store)
1/2 cup cooking oil
1 egg
1 3/4 cup water or broth

Place all ingredients in large bowl. Blend. Mix together egg, oil and water. Add these ingredients to the dry ingredients and mix until all ingredients are well blended. Divide dough in thirds. On floured surface, roll out to 1/4" thick. Cut out dog bones shapes. (Optional -- prick tops three times with toothpick.) Place on well oiled baking sheet. Bake at 325 degrees F for 25-30 minutes. Biscuits should be well browned on the bottom. Don't store in an airtight container.

Meat Loaf With Apple Sauce

1 pound lean ground beef
3/4 pound pork sausages (remove casings)
1/2 teaspoon sage
1 tablespoon Worcestershire sauce
1/2 teaspoon garlic
2 cups canned apple sauce
1 1/2 cups very dry dog food
4 twists of pepper mill

Mix all of the ingredients together in the order in which they are given. Butter a loaf tin and pack them into it. Bake in a 350° F. oven for 45 minutes. This delicious meat loaf is excellent served on long day trips with your best friend.

Lima Bean, Rice and Hamburger Loaf
(a good energy recipe)

1 pound hamburger
1/2 teaspoon paprika
1/2 cup chopped onion
1/2 teaspoon garlic
1/4 teaspoon pepper
1 tablespoon parsley flakes
1 cup uncooked rice
2 small cans lima beans, drained
1 cup stock, or 2 bouillon cubes dissolved in 1 cup water
1 can condensed tomato soup

Sauté the hamburger in a skillet until it loses its reddish color. Add the paprika and the chopped onion and continue to cook over low heat for 5 minutes longer. Then remove from heat. Add the garlic, pepper and parsley flakes; stir in the uncooked rice just as it comes from the package. Last, stir in the lima beans, stock and tomato soup. Take care not to break up the lima beans.
Place the mixture in a well-greased loaf tin and bake at 350° F. for 45 minutes, or until the center of the loaf is firm.

Madrid Rice Casserole

3 slices bacon, cut into 1/4" pieces
1/2 cup onion, chopped fine
1 1/2 pounds hamburger
1/4 teaspoon thyme
1/4 teaspoon sweet basil
1 small can tomato juice
1 1/2 cups precooked rice
1 green pepper, cut into 1/4" pieces
1/2 teaspoon paprika

Sauté the bacon in a skillet until slightly browned. Pour away most of the fat; add the onion and continue to sauté until the onion is slightly transparent. Add the hamburger to the onion and bacon, along with the thyme and basil. Cook for a few minutes longer, until the meat loses its reddish color. Remove from heat, and add the tomato juice. Stir in the rice just as it comes from the package. Add most of the green pepper, reserving a few pieces for later. Place the entire mixture in a 1 1/2 quart casserole and sprinkle the paprika over the top. Place the casserole in a 350° F. oven and bake for 35 minutes, uncovered. Five minutes before removing from the oven, sprinkle the remaining green pepper over the top for color. Serve right from the casserole used to bake in.
I usually bake a double quantity of this casserole, one for serving and one for freezing.

Variations:
Add 1 package frozen okra
Add 1 package frozen zucchini squash
Add 1 package frozen French-style green beans

Some of these recipes you can dine with your best friend. We do!

Veal Breast Stuffed With Hamburger

My dog's biggest complaint about economy dishes like stuffed veal breast is that they want more meat. Here is a recipe that has economy and plenty of meat, too.

1 3-pound veal breast
1 pound hamburger
2 cups moist bread crumbs
1 medium onion, chopped very fine
1 tablespoon paprika

Have your butcher make a pocket in the veal breast. If you purchase meats in a market where they are prepackaged, you can do this yourself with a very sharp paring knife. Just slice a pocket midway between the top and bottom of the veal breast. It should be large enough to hold the meat and other stuffing ingredients.
Mix the hamburger with the onions and bread crumbs, and stuff this mixture into the pocket. Fasten the end with skewers, Sprinkle the paprika all over the outside of the veal breast and place in a shallow roasting pan. Cover with foil for the first half of the cooking time. Roast at 350° F. For 1 hour. Then remove foil and bake uncovered for 45 minutes more. The veal should become a rich brown color.
You can make a delicious gravy from the pan juices. Remove the meat to a heated platter. Add 1/2 cup water to the pan juices, and thicken with a heaping tablespoon of flour dissolved in another 1/4 cup of water.

Egg-Burger Surprises

1 pound hamburger
1/2 teaspoon garlic
1/4 teaspoon pepper
1/4 cup instant flour
6 hard-cooked eggs, peeled and cooled
1 raw egg, slightly beaten
1 cup dry bread crumbs or 1 cup crushed shredded wheat
Vegetable oil for deep frying

Mix the hamburger, garlic, pepper and flour until smooth.
Form into 6 large patties, and place a hard-cooked egg in the
center of each. Bring up the sides of each patty and form into
a covering all around the egg. Brush with the slightly beaten
egg and roll in the bread crumbs or shredded wheat.
Drop into hot fat and fry until the patties turn golden brown.
Drain on paper towel. Cut each patty in half when serving.
Leave half of the egg in each section. These can be served
cold.

Lazaro's Hamburger Meat Pudding

1 pound hamburger
3 eggs, separated
4 strips bacon, cut into 1/4" pieces
1/4 cup milk
1 cup soft bread crumbs
1 tablespoon brandy (optional)
1/4 teaspoon lemon rind
1 tablespoon parsley, chopped fine
1/4 teaspoon pepper
2 tablespoons butter

Place the hamburger in a mixing bowl and add the egg yolks.
Add the bacon, milk and bread crumbs. Add the brandy,
lemon rind, parsley and pepper. Mix all very well.
Beat the egg whites until they are stiff and dry. Fold them into
the meat mixture. Brush a ring mold generously with the
butter and carefully spoon in the meat mixture. Try not to
pack it too tightly. Place the ring mold in a pan of water and
bake in a 350° F. oven for 50 minutes, or until firmly set.

PET SAFETY

Safe Handling Instructions

- For your protection, follow these safe handling instructions.

- Keep food refrigerated or frozen.

- Thaw in refrigerator or microwave.

- Cook thoroughly.

- Some food products may contain bacteria that could cause illness if the product is mishandled or cooked improperly.

- Keep raw meat and poultry separate from other foods.

- Keep hot foods hot.

- Refrigerate leftovers immediately or discard.

- Wash working surfaces (including cutting boards), utensils and hands after touching raw meat or poultry.

POISONING

<u>General Remarks</u>
A poison is any substance harmful to the body. Animal baits are palatable poisons that encourage ingestion. This makes them an obvious choice for intentional poisoning.

Dogs by nature are curious and have a tendency to hunt small game, or explore out of the way places such as wood piles, weed thickets, and storage ports. This puts them into contact with insects, dead animals and toxic plants. It also means that in many cases of suspected poisoning the actual agent will be unknown. The great variety of potentially poisonous plants and shrubs makes the identification difficult or impossible--unless the owner has direct knowledge that his dog has eaten a certain plant or product. Most cases suspected of being malicious poisoning actually are not.

In some types of vegetation only certain parts of the plant are toxic. In others, all parts are poisonous. Ingestion causes a wide range of symptoms. They include mouth irritation, drooling, vomiting, diarrhea, hallucinations, seizures, coma and death. Other plant substances cause skin rash. Some toxic plants have specific pharmacological actions, which are used in medicines.

Tables of toxic plants, shrubs, and trees are included for reference.

POISONOUS HOUSEPLANTS

Toxic House Plants

A. That give rash after contact with skin or mouth:

Chrysanthemum	Creeping fig
Cheeping fig	Poinsettia
Spider mum might	Pot mum
produce dermatitis	

B. Irritating (toxic oxalates), especially the mouth gets swollen; tongue pain; sore lips:

Arrowhead vine	Majesty
Boston ivy	Neththytis Ivy
Caladium	Pathos
Brunk Cane	Red princess
Emerald Duke	Saddle leaf
Heart leaf (Philodendron)	(Philodendron)
Marble Queen	Split leaf (Philodendron)

C. Toxic plants -- may contain wide variety of poisons. Most cause vomiting, abdominal pain and cramps. Some cause tremors, heart and/or kidney problems, which are difficult for owner to interpret:

Amaryllis	Ivy
Asparagus fern	Jerusalem Cherry
Azalea	Needlepoint Ivy
Bird of paradise	Pot mum
Creeping Charlie	Ripple Ivy
Crown of thorns	Spider mum
Elephant ears	Sprangeri Fern
Glocal Ivy	Umbrella plant
Heart Ivy	

OUTDOOR PLANTS WITH TOXIC EFFECTS

A. Outdoor plants that produce vomiting and diarrhea in some cases:

Delphinium   Ground cherry
Daffodil   Fox glove
Castor bean   Larkspur
Indian Turnip   Indian Tobacco
Skunk Cabbage   Wisteria
Poke Weed   Soap berry
Bittersweet woody

B. Trees and shrubs which are poisonous and may produce vomiting, abdominal pain, and in some cases diarrhea:

Horse Chestnut   Mock orange
Buckeye   Bird of Paradise bush
Rain Tree   Black locust
Monkey Pod   Apricot, almond
American Yew   Peach, cherry
English Yew   Wild cherry
Western Yew   Japanese plum
English Holly   Balsam pear
Privet

C. Outdoor plants with varied toxic effect:

Rhubarb   Dologeton
Sunburned potatoes   Buttercup
Tomato vine   Nightshade
Loco weed   Poison Hemlock
Lupine   Jimson weed

Pig weed
Water Hemlock
Mushrooms
Moonseed
May apple

Dutchman's breeches
Mescal bean
Angel's Trumpet
Jasmine
Matrimony vine

D. Hallucinogens:
Marijuana
Morning glory
Periwinkle

Peyote
Nutmeg
Loco weed

E. Convulsions:
China berry
Coriaria
Moonweed
Nux vomica
Water Hemlock

Wording of Pet Food Labels
(including a handy definition list)

One pet food company advertises their food as better than others do because the main ingredient in their food is poultry meat and others use feathers. But when we read the labels on all the different pet foods we can't find "feathers" listed as an ingredient in any of them. The words used on pet food labels can hide many evils. They are sometimes misunderstood, often ignored and can be confusing. To limit confusion when listing each ingredient in a food, all pet food companies should be required to also use the International Feed Number (IFN) that has been assigned to each feed grade ingredient. Then we would clearly identify the ingredients in each pet food and be able to make intelligent choices among them. To help you determine what may be in the pet food you are now buying, here are definitions of some words that can be found on most pet food labels today:

By-product: An ingredient produced in the course of making a primary food ingredient; a secondary or incidental product. Feathers are a by-product of poultry meat processing. Feathers which are removed from a carcass during production of poultry meat is then hydrolyzed (pressure cooked with steam until they are an edible gel) which makes them an acceptable feed grade ingredient. Hydrolyzed feathers have been assigned the (IFN) International Feed Number 5-03-795 and can appear on a label as "Poultry By-products". On page 158 in the AAFCO book *Official Publication, 1994, Association Feed Control Officials Incorporated*, they show: "Hydrolyzed Poultry By-products Aggregate is the product resulting from heat treatment, or a combination thereof, of all by-products of slaughter poultry, clean and undercomposed, including such parts as heads, feet, underdeveloped eggs, intestines, feathers and blood." The IFN assigned to this mix is 5-14-508. Today's regulations allow the entire mix or any part of it to appear on a label as "Poultry By-products." A "Fish By-product" can contain heads, tails, intestines and blood. This fish process residue has been assigned the IFN 5-07-977. A "Meat By-product" could be viscera and blood soaked sawdust from the floors of a packing house or any other source. Each one has its own IFN. Some of the animal feed IFN's that contain wood shavings from the floor of a processing facility include "Dried Ruminant Waste" #1-07-526, and "Undried Processed Animal Waste Products" #5-02-790. It is important to note that the amount of wood shavings in either of these two "Meat By-products" is limited and should not be more than 35% in one and 40% in the other. When a pet food label's list of ingredients shows the word By-product you can be assured that there is NO measurable amount of meat in the ingredient. If the ingredient contained enough meat that it could be measured the pet food company would proudly list the MEAT, not just the By-product of that meat's production.

Mill Run: An ingredient consisting of residue left after the primary food product has been extracted during a milling process. A "Corn Mill Run" would be a pulverized blend of cornhusk and cobs, which are left after a milling process has removed the kernels. Mill Run is the vegetable or produce equivalent of meat's By-product.

Digest: An animal feed-grade ingredient that must be made soluble with the use of heat and moisture. Since these the ingredients are not soluble in their natural state they require this manufacturing process before they can be put into pet food. An example of this would be the feet of poultry IFN 5-07-947. When a pet food label shows "Poultry Digest" as an ingredient this could be what is in the food.

Meal: A ground or pulverized composite of animal feed-grade ingredients. One example of a Meal is found on page 156 in AAFCO book, Official Publication, 1994, Association of American Feed Control Officials Incorporated. It shows "Poultry By-product Meal consists of the ground, rendered, clean parts of the carcass of slaughtered poultry, such as necks, feet, underdeveloped eggs, and intestines, exclusive of feathers, except in such amounts as might occur unavoidably in good processing practices." The IFN for this blend is 5-03-795. The only MEAT that might be in Poultry By-product Meal" 5-03-795 is what could be left on the necks after becoming clean rendered By-products of meat production. This is not enough that it can be measured and thus have an ingredient listing showing any POULTRY MEAT to be in food.

Gluten: The sticky substance in wheat or cornstarch that gives the starch its tough elastic quality. It is used to hold together the pulverized composite of animal feed-grade ingredients.

Digestibility Test: A test to see how much time it takes a food solid to break down in a strong laboratory acid. There are companies that are claiming the food, which passes this test in the shortest amount of time, provides the best nutrition for all animals. But the word digestibility is not a synonym for the word nutritious. Just because a food solid can be broken down in an acid does not mean the animal eating it can nutritionally use that kind of food. Not all dogs or cats have the same nutritional acceptance of any one-food source. This has been established in tests cited in the 1985 *Nutrient Requirements of Dogs* by the National Research Council. Since pet foods are made from many different food sources we could thus be making the proverbial comparison between apples and oranges. It would be a mistake to judge any food's total nutritive value on one test demonstrating how fast it breaks down in laboratory acid. Comparing pet foods by using a Digestibility Test is valid only if the foods being tested are of equal nutritional value for the animal that will be eating them. Then the faster a food breaks down the easier it is for the animals' digestive system to make use of it.

Today, pet food labeling is done using the honor system. The AAFCO claims to be the governing body of the pet food industry, and has tried to get some form of standardization (see the quotes above). But even the terms of The AAFCO wants are so vague that two different foods could be made with two different ingredients and have the same term on their labels. The ingredients going into pet foods today have no clear single set of label terms with a precise set of definitions attached. If pet food products used the IFN with each ingredient listed we would know if a food contained Dehydrated swine excreta (IFN 5-02-790) or Hydrolyzed hair (IFN 5-08-997) as a "Meat By-product" or if the ingredient identified as "Poultry By-product" was feet (IFN 5-07-947) or feathers (IFN 5-03-795). Unfortunately, until we get new labeling regulations requiring the use of IFN's, pet food buyers will remain at the mercy of competing pet food companies to tell them what is in their food.

I believe laws should be passed that would require all commercial animal feeds to use IFN numbers along with the wording they now use to list the ingredients in their product. That would give us all a way to know what is in their food. I also have a suggestion of what can be done until all animal feeds are labeled with the IFN numbers. If you are now buying a pet food with words you don't understand on the label you might try this: contact the manufacturer and ask them for their definitions. If they do not give them to you in words you, the buyer, can understand, then maybe it's time to consider home cooking your pet's food. You'd know what was in the food, and for thousands of years before commercial pet food was available (just 75 years ago), that's what pet owners successfully did.

Frostbite:
Remove ice and snow from your pet's paws and coat at once. Frostbitten skin may turn reddish, white or gray, and it may be scaly or sloughing. If you suspect frostbite, take your pet to a warm place immediately. Thaw out frostbitten areas slowly by applying warm, moist towels that are changed frequently. Continue until the affected areas become flushed. Contact your veterinarian as soon as possible; he/she will probably want to evaluate the seriousness of the condition.

Snow Removal Salt:
Some substances produced to melt ice and snow have low to moderate toxicity, depending on the ingredients and amount ingested. Read the labels and take necessary precautions. Keep these products stored in tight containers out of your pet's and children's reach and be sure to remove salt from your pet's paws immediately.

Antifreeze:

Even a very small amount of antifreeze can be fatal. Precautions are necessary with all antifreeze products on the market. Read labels and warnings carefully. Thoroughly clean up spills at once. Keep containers closed tightly and store them where pets cannot get to them.

Napping Cats:

Cats sometimes climb onto vehicle engines for warmth. Before starting your vehicle, knock on the hood and honk the horn. Even if your own cat does not have access to your vehicle, a neighbor's cat might have taken shelter there.

Food:

Staying warm requires extra calories, so feed your pet accordingly when the temperature drops. Talk to your veterinarian for advice on feeding your pet.

Water:

Always have fresh, clean water available for your pet. If your pet is kept outdoors, be sure to check his water frequently since it may freeze.

NAMING YOUR PET

Seazar's Names For Boys

Abdul	Barclay	Brick
Abel	Barnard	Brock
Ace	Barney	Bruce
Adon	Baron	Bruno
Aki	Barton	Buck
Alban	Basil	Bundy
Aldo	Baxter	Burney
Alex	Bayley	Burt
Alf	Beal	Byrd
Alfie	Beamer	Caesar
Ali	Bear	Cal
Alroy	Beck	Callan
Alvin	Ben	Calvin
Ambler	Bennett	Carlos
Amis	Benson	Carlton
Amos	Bentley	Carson
Ang	Bernard	Casey
Angus	Bert	Cash
Anwar	Blackmore	Casper
Anwell	Blair	Cassidy
Apollo	Blane	Chad
Archie	Blaze	Chadwick
Argus	Bo	Chance
Aries	Bogart	Chang
Armstrong	Bolton	Chapin
Asa	Booker	Charles
Augie	Boone	Chet
Austin	Boston	Chuck
Avery	Brady	Cian
Axel	Bram	Clay
Bailey	Braxton	Clayton
Baldwin	Brett	Cole

Colt	Dodge	Fane
Connie	Dory	Fay
Conway	Dover	Felix
Cooper	Dow	Fergus
Cort	Doyle	Fidel
Cotton	Drake	Finn
Crawford	Drew	Fisher
Crockett	Driscoll	Fletcher
Crosby	Dudley	Flint
Cruz	Duke	Flip
Cuba	Dustin	Fortune
Dag	Dutch	Fox
Dagwood	Earl	Fraser
Dakota	Earnest	Fritz
Dale	Eaton	Gage
Dallan	Edgar	Gallagher
Dallas	Edson	Garett
Dalton	Edwin	Gaston
Daly	Eldon	Gavin
Damon	Eleazar	Gaylord
Daniel	Ellis	George
Darby	Elmo	Geronimo
Darton	Elmore	Gideon
Darwin	Elsworth	Gil
Dean	Elton	Gilby
Dedrick	Elwood	Gomer
Denver	Emilio	Granger
Denzel	Esmond	Grant
Derek	Estes	Grayson
Devon	Evan	Griffin
Dexter	Evander	Guido
Diamond	Ewing	Gus
Dirk	Ezra	Guy
Dixon	Fagan	Hal

Haley	Judge	Magnus
Hamlet	Jules	Manfred
Hannibal	Julius	Marcus
Hans	Justis	Mario
Hansel	Kai	Marmaduke
Hardy	Keegan	Marsh
Harley	Keelan	Maximillian
Harper	Kemper	Mel
Harris	Kennedy	Merlin
Hawk	Kerby	Miller
Heathcliff	Kermit	Mohammad
Hilton	Kerrigan	Monroe
Hobart	King	Morgan
Hogan	Kipp	Moses
Homer	Kirk	Murphey
Horatio	Knight	Murray
Hugh	Lacy	Myles
Hugo	Ladd	Napoleon
Hunter	Laird	Nash
Igor	Lamont	Nelson
Ike	Lance	Nemo
Indi	Lane	Nick
Ishmael	Larz	Nico
Jackson	Lawford	Nino
Jagger	Lennox	Noah
Jantu	Leo	Noble
Jasper	Leeroy	Nunzio
Jed	Lex	Obadiah
Jedediah	Link	Olle
Jericho	Linus	Oliver
Jesse	Lucas	Ollie
Ji	Luke	Omar
Jonah	Luther	O'Neal
Jordon	Lyle	Orson
Josiah	Mac	Orville

Oscar	Rex	Sheldon
Otis	Rhett	Shem
Otto	Rider	Shep
Owen	Riley	Sherlock
Paco	Rochester	Shiloh
Paine	Rollo	Sidney
Palmer	Romeo	Sigmund
Paolo	Roper	Simon
Parker	Rory	Sinclair
Pascal	Roscoe	Skipp
Patton	Ross	Sky
Paxton	Royal	Slade
Pearce	Royce	Solomon
Percy	Rufus	Sparky
Pierre	Rusty	Stanley
Plato	Ryder	Starling
Polk	Saber	Starr
Porter	Salem	Sterling
Presley	Samson	Stone
Prince	Sanders	Storm
Quan	Sany	Stuart
Quincy	Sanford	Styles
Quinn	Sargent	Sven
Radcliff	Sawyer	Tab
Rafael	Scully	Tanner
Raleigh	Sebastian	Tate
Rance	Sedgewick	Tavey
Ranger	Seger	Taylor
Ransom	Sequoia	Teddy
Raven	Serafin	Tennyson
Reece	Shamus	Thor
Reggie	Shandy	Thorpe
Rene	Shane	Timon
Reuben	Shelby	Tito

Tobias	Wade	Worth
Trainor	Waite	Wylie
Trigg	Waldo	Xander
True	Walker	Xenos
Tucker	Webster	Yang
Tully	West	Yates
Turner	Whitman	Yeats
Ty	Wiley	Yin
Tyrone	Willard	York
Ugo	Win	Yoshi
Ulysses	Winston	Zack
Valentine	Winter	Zander
Vance	Wolfe	Zeke
Vaughan	Woody	Zeus

Cleopatra's Names For Girls

Adelaide	Candy	Earlene
Adina	Carita	Eartha
Adora	Carmel	Ebony
Aisha	Chandler	Echo
Alexis	Chanel	Edrea
Allegra	Chantal	Effie
Almira	Charity	Electra
Amaris	Chiquita	Ellamay
Amber	Chloe	Elvira
Amethyst	Cleo	Emerald
Anastasia	Colette	Emmylou
Anouk	Comfort	Epiphany
Aphrodite	Consuela	Esmerelda
Aretha	Coral	Eve
Ariel	Cordelia	Fae
Asher	Crystal	Faline
Astra	Cybil	Fanny
Astrid	Cyrena	Fate
Autumn	Daisy	Fawn
Bambi	Delfina	Felicity
Bathsheba	Delilah	Feodora
Bebe	Demetria	Fifi
Beulah	Desdemona	Flora
Bliss	Devotion	Fortune
Blossom	Diantha	Fritzie
Blythe	Dilys	Gabey
Bonita	Disa	Gay
Brandy	Dodi	Georgia
Cally	Dolly	Gertrude
Cameo	Dorinda	Gigi
Camella	Drew	Gilda
Candida	Dusty	Ginger

Giselle	Kenya	Melly
Glenda	Kirby	Meoldy
Golda	Kit	Mercedes
Goldie	Kitty	Mia
Grace	Klarissa	Midori
Gypsy	Kylie	Missy
Haley	Lani	Misty
Happy	Laverne	Mitzi
Harper	Letitia	Modesty
Hazel	Libby	Mom
Holly	Lilith	Morgan
Honey	Lily	Nadia
Hope	Lizzy	Nadine
Hunter	Lorelei	Nattie
Ingrid	Lotus	Nevada
Iris	Lucy	Nikki
Isadora	Lulu	Nina
Ivana	Mabel	Nixie
Ivory	Mackenzie	Noel
Ivy	Maddie	Nollie
Jade	Madison	Nova
Jasmine	Madonna	Odelia
Jericho	Maggie	Ollie
Herri	Mandy	Onyx
Hewel	Maribel	Opal
Jo	Marigolde	Pandora
Jolene	Marilyn	Pansy
Juliet	Maris	Patience
Kassie	Marni	Patsy
Kat	Martha	Pearl
Kateri	Mathilda	Penelope
Keely	Maxine	Penny
Keiki	Maya	Peony
Keisha	Melanie	Pepita
Kennedy	Mel	Pepper

Perry	Rumer	Tawny
Petra	Sable	Teddi
Petula	Sabrina	Temperance
Petunia	Sacha	Tempest
Pippy	Sade	Tessa
Phoebe	Sadie	Tiffany
Phoenix	Saffron	Tipper
Polly	Sage	Toby
Poppy	Salem	Topaz
Precious	Salena	Torrey
Pricious	Samantha	Trixie
Priscilla	Sapphire	Trudy
Prissy	Scarlett	Umeko
Prudence	Season	Unity
Prudy	Shannon	Ursula
Queenie	Sheba	Vega
Ray	Shiloh	Velvet
Rain	Sidney	Venus
Randy	Sissy	Vera
Raven	Sky	Vern
Reba	Spring	Veronica
Regan	Stella	Vida
Reiko	Storm	Violet
Rennae	Sukie	Virtue
Rxexana	Summer	Vonnie
Rhoda	Tabby	Wendy
Riley	Tabitha	Whitley
Romy	Taffy	Willow
Rosamund	Tallulah	Wilma
Rosanna	Tamara	Winnie
Rose	Tammy	Winona
Ruby	Tate	Winter

Xandra	Yvette	Zowie
Xaviera	Yvonne	Zona
Xena	Zabrina	Zora
Ying	Zelda	Zowie
Yoko	Zinnia	Zuleika
Ysabel	Zoe	

COSMIC COMPATIBILITY
(HOROSCOPE)

BY: NANCY WELCH

Aries March 21-April 20

If you have a little darling born under this star sign, the name "Sweet Pea" would be fitting (that is the flower of this star sign).

For a lonely person, choosing a pet born under this sign is a perfect choice. Most Aries are incredibly active and love physical attention. Beware however that they are also accident prone and mischievous.

Obedience school is a plus for this pet, but still a good choice of pet because they are generous with affection and are fierce protectors!

Taurus April 21-May 21

Although stubborn like the bull depicted by this sign, this pet is basically and by nature very gentle.

When they do fight they put everything into it, this would make a fierce protector.

If they show no interest in learning something save your time and effort on something else or you'll see the stubborn side of their nature.

They are however very steadfast and loyal companions and will stay by you always.

Gemini May 22-June 21

Gemini's are very energetic and extremely inquisitive. This curious pet will keep you on your toes just trying to keep up with it. These traits make this the perfect pet for someone who likes to keep active but prefers to have company at the same time.

They do however love to hear their own voices so be prepared or forewarned whichever the case may be.

This pet will thoroughly investigate everything that you bring into its domain, then lose interest entirely.

When teaching them tricks, stick to one specific trick at a time and you'll be more successful.

Cancer June 22-July 23

Those born under this sign are of an extremely sensitive nature. It would be wise to instill a sense of security early on. These gentle loving souls are wonderful with people and have a very determined nature which makes them fast learners who respond well to love and affection.
These pets are nurturers as well as protectors.

Leo July 24-August 23

This pet absolutely loves to be the center of attention. They thrive on adoration, and demand praise, responding to it in everything that they do.
Be careful not to rein them too closely, without a little freedom you would break their confident spirit.
They are capable of learning anything with the proper amount of love and praise.

Virgo August 24-September 23

This pet, although shy will love to learn new tricks, and love you for teaching them.
You will find them extremely cooperative and accepting of routine and a sense or order.
If you are prone to schedules, this is your pet.

Libra September 24-October 23

If you want a pet to "show" or just show-off, this is the one! Their nature makes them accepting of being around others just like themselves (this is definitely not true of most signs). Although their natural confidence makes them receptive to show, you will need to work with them routinely on skills. Without this training a task that is unfamiliar will make them visibly frustrated.
These pets have peaceful, harmonious souls but tend to be prone to be moody.

Scorpio October 24-November 22

These powerful pets are gifted with intelligence and strong wills. They will guard your home with intense loyalty. They are quick to temper so will need to be taught control at an early age. (This can be a task because of their stubborn nature)! Their physical energy is in direct proportion to their strong personality, and they are constantly on the move.
With gentle guidance, this passionate pet is sure to capture your heart.

Sagittarius November 23-December 21

This pet is not only trusting, but very easy going and quick to love everyone. Don't expect him to guard your home because most likely they would welcome the company as long as they're given some attention.
This is an extremely curious animal and loves freedom when it can get it. This spirited soul loves the outdoors and to run. They also make great nurturers.

Capricorn December 22-January 20

Behind the quiet demeanor of this pet is an active, ambitious soul with a remarkable strong will.
They will have definite likes and dislikes, and will be quick to make them known to you.
They are a loyal and loving pet that learn well with rewards. They do not like to share their spotlight with another pet.

Aquarius January 21-February 19

This is a social creature. Companionships are important and they will be well received by others. You'll find that there will always be offers and request to "take them off your hands". Their stubbornness is most effectively handled with affection. These tend to be indoor pets and they love to be pampered. They approach physical and outdoor activity reluctantly.

Pisces February 20-March 20

This pet is extremely sensitive to outside influences and therefore will be easy to teach with consistency. They are receptive in nature and easy going. They may however always require a leash, left to themselves, their dreamy nature makes them roamers and they may forget to come home!

PLANNED
PARENTHOOD

Puppy Planning

You can expect to pay these estimated expenses during the first year of your puppy's life. Variances within geographical areas should be expected. Some are one-time purchases, such as a sturdy crate. Others are annual expenses, including general veterinary expenses and heartworm preventative. Items with a "*" are helpful, optional items and are not included in the first-year totals.

Annual Expenses

	Small Dog	Large Dog
Pad for crate	$15	$50
Cover for pet bed	$20	$40
Various chew toys	$30	$30
Dental kit (toothbrush and paste)	$6	$6
Dog shampoo	$20	$35
Routine veterinary care	$250	$250
*Boarding at kennel (based on 2 week vacation)	$120	$240
Premium dog food	$100	$500

ESSENTIAL EXPENSES

	SMALL DOG	LARGE
DOG		
Folding Crate	$65	$150
Dog Bed	$40	$75
(with removable cover)		
Plastic Doghouse	$50	$90
Baby Gates (2)	$80	$80
Dog Bowls (2)	$10	$40
(Ceramic or No-Tip Stainless Steel)		
Collars, Adjustable (2)	$10	$20
Nylon Harness	$10	$20
Leash, 6-foot	$9	$9
Identification Tag	$5	$5
Toenail Clippers & Styptic Powder	$10	$17
Grooming Brushes, Gloves,	$20	$20
Combs, Scissors		
(Equipment varies w/breed)		
Yard Scoop	$15	$18
Anti-Chewing Spray	$7	$7
Pet Stain & Odor Remover	$20	$20
(1 Gallon)		
Fencing for Yard	$300	$300
Electric or 6-foot	$1,000	$1,000
Privacy Fence		
(Dependent on size of yard)		
Vehicle Barrier	$50	$50
(Dependent on style and size of vehicle)		
Spay/Neuter	$70	$114
	$285	$500
Puppy Exams	$85	$85
Vaccines	$140	$140
Heartworm Preventive	$75	$120
Flea & Tick Control	$35	$75
(Year Round)		

Obedience Classes	$200	$200
(10 Months)	$500+	$500+
Travel Crate	$30	$130
(For Airline Use)		
Pet Door	$50	$100
	$140	$180

**TOTAL ESTIMATED
EXPENSES FOR PUPPY'S
FIRST YEAR :**   **$1,807**   **$2896**

FROM THE HEART

SEAZAR & CLEO'S WORDS OF WISDOM

FRIENDSHIP HAS NO NAME BUT LOVE.
SAHABIB

WHEN YOU MAKE NEW FRIENDS, DON'T FORGET THE
OLD; ONE IS BLACK THE OTHER GOLD.
ERASMUS

THE THINGS OUR FRIENDS DO WITH US AND FOR US
FORM A PORTION OF OUR LIVES; THEY STRENGTHEN
OUR PERSONALITY.
GOETHE

"STAY" IS A CHARMING WORD IN A FRIEND'S
VOCABULARY.
AMOS BRONSON ALCOTT

FRIENDSHIP IS ONE OF THE GREATEST LUXURIES OF
LIFE.
EDWARD EVERETT HALE

FRIENDSHIP IS A SHELTERING TREE.
SAMUEL TAYLOR COLERIDGE

WHEN WE LOSE A FRIEND WE DIE A LITTLE.
LOUISA BOOTH

ACTIONS, NOT WORDS, ARE THE TRUE CRITERIA OF
THE ATTACHMENT OF FRIENDS.
GEORGE WASHINGTON

A FRIEND IS THE ONE WHO COMES IN WHEN THE
WHOLE WORLD HAS GONE OUT.

HOLD A TRUE FRIEND WITH BOTH YOUR HANDS.
NIGERIAN PROVERB

A CONSTANT FRIEND IS A THING RARE AND HARD TO FIND.
PLUTARCH

A FRIEND THINKS OF YOU WHEN ALL OTHERS ARE THINKING OF THEMSELVES.

THE BETTER PART OF ONE'S LIFE CONSISTS OF HIS FRIENDSHIPS.
ABRAHAM LINCOLN

A FRIEND IS A GIFT YOU GIVE YOURSELF.
ROBERT LOUIS STEVENSON

WHO, BEING LOVED, IS POOR?
OSCAR WILDE

A FAITHFUL FRIEND IS THE MEDICINE OF LIFE.
APOCRYPHA

THERE'S NOTHING WORTH THE WEAR OF WINNING, BUT LAUGHTER AND THE LOVE OF FRIENDS.
HILAIRE BELLOC

REPROVE A FRIEND IN SECRET, BUT PRAISE HIM BEFORE OTHERS.
LEONARDO DA VINCI

NO MAN IS USELESS WHILE HE HAS A FRIEND.
ROBERT L. STEVENSON

A FRIEND MUST NOT BE INJURED, EVEN IN JEST.
SYRUS

DID YOU KNOW?

Why do dogs eat grass?

Either the dog has an upset stomach, or they lack something in their diet. On some occasions, a dog will eat grass to induce vomiting.

Why do dogs roll in...?

Dogs have a keen sense of smell and most are very territorial. Every deposit on the ground is like a marker for that particular dog so when another dog smells the material, it knows that another dog has been in the area. They will roll in the material as a means of applying their own scent in the area to discourage other dogs.

The Simple Truths

While the short list of what dogs do is not complete, it would be unfair to end without mentioning the aspects of canine behavior we do understand.

1. Dogs sleep as often as possible.

2. Dogs charge ferociously at the door whenever your house is attacked by Girl Scouts, newspaper and letter carriers or meter readers.

3. Dogs hang around people who give them treats.

4. Dogs eat anything that was once living and many things that are plainly inedible.

5. Dogs get bored without regular mental stimulation.

6. Dogs do not like to be confined away from those they love.

7. Dogs curl up by your feet.

8. Dogs kiss when given the opportunity.

9. Dogs fetch balls until we are exhausted of playing fetch.

10. Dogs give us the opportunity to display all that is good in human beings-compassion, empathy, charity, humor, strength, responsibility and, most of all, love.

HOMEMADE PET TOOTHPASTE:
Care as much about your pets teeth as your own

Not all animals respond well to pet toothpaste. If your pet is hard to please, try these unconventional flavors.

Garlic:
Add a bit of garlic to lukewarm water and use that to moisten the brush. I think dogs and cats must be part Italian - They seem to love garlic.

Bouillon:
If garlic doesn't tickle his taste buds, or if you can't stand having a pet with garlic breath, dip the brush in chicken or beef broth. Nothing beats the effectiveness of a good toothpaste, but at least this may help your pet accept a brushing.

Reasons to Brush Your Dog's Teeth

1. It is unequivocally the best means of preventing periodontal disease.

2. Bacteria from gum infections from lack of daily brushing can spread to vital organs and cause damage.

3. Daily brushing will help decrease the number of times your dog will need to be anesthetized for a professional cleaning.

4. You will save your dog's teeth and money because you'll have fewer bills for professional cleanings or periodontal therapy.

5. Close encounters with your dog will be more pleasant. Brushing keeps breath smelling fresher.

6. Your dog will be happier because it will be able to enjoy eating and playing fetch with you.

7. Your dog will live a longer, healthier life.

NOT KEEPING YOUR PET'S TEETH AND GUMS
HEALTHY. Dental problems are the number one pet health
concern of veterinarians today. The proverbial "doggie
breath" is not just an annoyance, but is often the sign of a
painful problem lurking beneath the surface of the gums that
can slowly poison your pet.

OVERFEEDING YOUR PET. Face it. We love our pets like
children and we like to indulge them with food...and lots of it.
Too often, however, we're killing them with kindness. To
veterinarians overweight pets are like tubby time bombs, with
each extra ounce of body fat ticking away at a pet's longevity,
vitality and mobility.

The Case For Neutering
Why the surgery is good for your pet.

To neuter or not to neuter? Unless you're planning to breed your cat or dog, most experts wholeheartedly support this surgery. Here's why:

1. It can prevent disease. Neutering reduces the risk of infection and cancer in pets' reproductive organs. So they'll stay healthy and may live longer.

2. It keeps down the population. There aren't enough homes for all the pets in our shelters right now, let alone those not yet born.

3. It won't make them less protective. Neutering won't turn your watchdog into a wimp. The procedure has no effect on a dog's basic instinct to defend its territory. What's more, most neutered pets are more loving and responsive to their owners, since they're no longer preoccupied with mating.

4. Each year, in the United States alone, more than 8 million surplus dogs and cats are destroyed because there are not enough homes for all of them.
5. Euthanizing 8 million dogs and cats is a $300 million annual tax burden.
6. Only 1 out of every 10 cats, and 2 out of every 8 dogs ever find a permanent, loving home.
7. of the animals turned in to animal shelters are owner-relinquished.
8. of the animals turned in to animal shelters are purebred.
9. of the dogs hit by automobiles are unaltered males.
10. One unaltered female dog and her offspring can produce 67,000 dogs in six years. One unaltered female cat and her offspring can produce 420,000 cats in six years.
11. The majority of dog bites on postal carriers are inflicted by unaltered male dogs.
12. Female dogs and cats altered before they are one year old are 99.9% less likely to experience several types of reproductive cancer.
13. On average, altered animals live longer, healthier lives.
14. Spayed and neutered animals present far fewer behavioral problems in the home.
15. In most cities and counties, pet licensing fees are considerably lower for altered animals.
16. As a result of advances in veterinary medicine, kittens and puppies can safely be altered at as early as 10 weeks of age.
17. Please remember to get your dogs and cats spayed or neutered.

NOT EXERCISING YOUR PET. You must give sufficient exercise for the "breed need". Pets need exercise to keep in top physical condition and to keep from getting "hardening of the attitudes." When you're out of the yard, keep your pet on a leash. If you can't go outside with them, you at least have to provide them with physical and mental stimulation indoors.

Lessen The Loneliness for Home-Alone Pets

Every day, millions of pet owners head off to work or school, leaving their furry friends at home. These pets spend many hours dividing their time between sleeping and playing. Although this lifestyle may sound like paradise, pets can and do become bored - sometimes resulting in destructive behavior. By making simple alterations to the home environment and providing the proper toys, owners can make a pet's leisure time more entertaining and enjoyable.

The Waltham Centre for Pet Care and Nutrition, based in Leicestershire, England, offers this advice for banishing boredom (and giving yourself a little more peace of mind when Fido has to fend for himself):

- Mount mirrors in the play areas of young animals. Not only is this amusing for the dog, it also helps in the pet's socialization.
- Choose toys that stimulate active, entertaining play, such as weighted balls that roll in unpredictable directions and rubber chew toys in various shapes and textures.
- Rotate the toys you leave with your pet so that each day it has a "new" toy.
- Consider a second pet if you leave your dog alone for extended periods of time. Dogs are pack animals and need companionship.
- Leave a radio or the television set on while you are out to keep your pet company.
- Install a doggie door so pets have access to an enclosed outdoor run or yard.
- Make sure indoor pets have access to a window or patio door so they can see outside.

Good or Bad?

Good Toys:

- Busy box toys
- Nylon or rubber chew toys
- Sturdy squeakier toys
- Dental-hygiene toys
- Bounce toys
- Flying discs
- Water-retrieval toys
- Washable toys
- Tug toys when played with properly

Bad Toys:
- Old shoes or socks
- Sticks
- Unwashable toys
- Overused toys
- Poorly made stuffed animals
- Poorly made squeakier toys
- Toys stuffed with nutshells or polystyrene beads
- Toys with ribbons or strings
- Children's toys
- Tug toys when played with improperly

Social Dogs Are Happy Dogs

A well-socialized dog is a happy dog, and good social skills start at a young age. As soon as your dog or pup is fully vaccinated, your whole family can begin exposing it to various stimuli, including people outside of its "family pack" and other dogs. (Pups without full immunity are at risk for contracting many life-threatening diseases, so hold off on outdoors until the vet tells you this is OK.) Dogs accustomed to encountering new sights, noises and people tend to be more relaxed and easier to live with.

You can begin your adventures together in your own neighborhood and extend them to parks, hiking trails, play groups, doggie day care outings and vacations. These all provide excellent opportunities for your dog to meet and greet all kinds of interesting and new species.

Puppy socials and obedience classes also are wonderful for socializing a dog. These activities can provide them with further training in addition to canine-to-canine interaction. Be forewarned, however, to leash your dog whenever you're out and about, even if you see other dogs off leash. Also, take care not to let people, especially children, rush toward your pet. This can startle a dog and evoke a flight or fight instinct. Additionally, allow your dog to contact only friendly and leashed dogs. Always supervise your dog's contact with other canines and people.

VETERINARIAN'S VOICE

1.) How old does my dog have to be to be neutered?
Approximately 6 months of age.

2.) My dog has loose stool. What do I do?
If it just started and is not associated with any other symptoms, then you can fast (no food) for 24 hours and give Pepto Bismol three times a day. Also when you resume feeding you can add boiled white rice to food. If it persists, call your veterinarian.

3.) How do I get a tick off of my dog?
We recommend that you use tweezers and grab it as close to the skin as possible and gently pull back.

4.) How can I stop my dog from chewing everything?
Exercise your dog each day so he's not so full of energy all the time. Supply him with plenty of chew toys so he doesn't chew on things you don't want him to.

5.) How much and how often should I feed my dog?
It really depends on the food, and the dog. While most adults only need to be fed once a day, puppies need to be fed at least twice a day. On the back of most dog food bags, it usually has a chart with your dog's weight on it so you can easily check how much you should feed your dog.

6.) Will my dog calm down if I neuter him/her?
Not necessarily. It will decrease sexual behavior and make males less likely to roam. Activity level is also determined by the personality of a certain breed. As a rule dogs usually calm down as they get older.

7.) Can my dog catch a cold from me?
No.

8.) Why does my dog have to destroy things when I'm gone?
It may be a separation anxiety or may be caused by boredom.

9.) What will happen if I get another dog?
They may not get along at first, but over time they usually become best friends. It also depends on the particular personalities and the home environment of the dogs.

10.) How does my dog get worms?
They can get worms from fleas or ingesting other dog's stool. Puppies get worms from their mothers.

11.) What does a dog require for vaccinations?
Distemper, kennel cough, rabies, and lyme disease. Give rabies vaccine every 1 to 3 years depending on which state you live in. Give a heartworm check once a year.

12.) What is a heartworm disease?
It is a blood parasite that dogs get from mosquitoes. Your dog should be tested once a year for heartworms and be on heartworm preventative (usually a monthly tablet) year round.

13.) Can dogs have heart attacks?
Dogs cannot have heart attacks, but they do get heart disease. Your dog should have a physical exam every year. This even includes having the veterinarian listen to your dog's heart.

14.) Is feeding people food to my dog harmful?
Once in a while it is a good treat, but it should never become a habit. Dog food which has all the vitamins, minerals, and nutrients your dog needs is a much better choice.

15.) How often should a dog get a bath?
Depending on how much time your dog spends outside, normally about once a month.

16.) I pulled a tick out of my dog but I think the head is still in there.
That's an old wives tale. This cannot happen. A small piece of a mouth part can get stuck, but this will be absorbed by the body and will not cause any problems.

17.) Are rawhides good for my dog?
Rawhides are okay as long as they are being supervised. They can swallow big chunks of it and also may cause gastro-intestinal problems.

Remember.....

Dogs
love you
no matter what!!

Recipes for a Happier Dog

1/2 mile walk
5 minute tug-o'-war with rope
5 mile car ride to pet store for treats
8 minute brushing
clean both ears
2 minute belly scratch, feed and let rest for an hour.

Weekend Recipe

1 mile walk downtown on leash to socialize with humans for
        good behavior
Go to a lake or ocean to let/learn to swim
After a fresh bowl of water, give a bath and dry with a 5
        minute brushing
Feed - relax

Dog Day Afternoon

Take to park to socialize with other dogs for an hour
With tennis ball, play fetch at least 15-20 minutes
Fresh bowl of water - bring with you
Stop at pet store to pick up a new toy or treats
10 minutes - spend time to teach new command
Brush teeth
Feed and both of you take a nap

My Best Friends Dog Recipe

_____
(Recipe Name)

Ingredients: (Abbreviations: pt. qt. pkg. c. tsp. T. ox. lb. gal. doz. sm. lg.)

_____   _____
_____   _____
_____   _____
_____   _____
_____   _____
_____   _____

Directions:_____
_____
_____
_____
_____
_____

Notes:_____
_____
_____

Name & Address (include pet name)

_____
_____
_____

Submit all entries to:
S.E.B.'s Market Place
16 Wentworth Terr.
Dover, NH 03820